everyday

fish & seafood

𝒫aRragon

Bath · New York · Singapore · Hong Kong · Cologne · Delhi · Melbourne

This edition published by Parragon in 2009

Parragon
Queen Street House
4 Queen Street
Bath BA1 1HE, UK

Copyright © Parragon Books Ltd 2008

ISBN 978-1-4075-7838-5

Printed in Indonesia

Designed by Terry Jeavons & Company

This book uses both metric and imperial measurements. Follow the same units of measurement throughout; do not mix metric and imperial. All spoon measurements are level: teaspoons are assumed to be 5ml, and tablespoons are assumed to be 15ml. Unless otherwise stated, milk is assumed to be full fat, eggs and individual vegetables are medium, and pepper is freshly ground black pepper.

The times given are an approximate guide only. Optional ingredients, variations or serving suggestions have not been included in the calculations.

Recipes using raw or very lightly cooked eggs should be avoided by infants, the elderly, pregnant women, convalescents, and anyone suffering from an illness. Pregnant and breastfeeding women are advised to avoid eating peanuts and peanut products. Sufferers from nut allergies should be aware that some of the ready-made ingredients used in the recipes in this book may contain nuts. Always check the packaging before use.

everyday fish&seafood

introduction

Fish has so many virtues that it is hard to know where to start listing them!

As a health food, fish is superb. It is high in first-class protein and low in salt. It contains vitamins, including A and D in oil-rich fish, and some of the B vitamins, as well as a whole range of minerals – iron, calcium, copper, magnesium, manganese, phosphorus, potassium, selenium, sodium, iodine, fluorine and zinc. White fish is low in fat, and the fat in fresh oil-rich fish such as halibut, swordfish, salmon, scallops and tuna contains high amounts of the polyunsaturated fats called omega-3 fatty acids. These fats are essential to health because they cannot be produced by the human body, and research shows that they reduce cholesterol absorption and help to lower blood-cholesterol levels, preventing the arteries from clogging and averting coronary heart disease.

Omega-3 fatty acids are also believed to help in the prevention of cancers of the breast, prostate and colon and reduce the inflammation associated with rheumatoid arthritis. They even improve brain function and decrease the risk of dementia, depression and poor memory.

Fish is the perfect food for today's lifestyle – it is quick and easy to cook and is both light and substantial. On top of all this, fish is good to eat! There is such an incredible variety of fish available, and so many interesting ways to cook it, that you might forget you are eating a highly nutritious superfood and simply focus on the delicious dishes that you can make with it. It can be cooked very simply – baked, roasted, grilled, pan-fried or stir-fried – or added to risottos, paellas, pasta, soups, stews, elegant tarts or homely potato-topped pies. The list is endless.

Whether you are eating fish for the sake of your health, or because you love the taste and convenience of it, enjoy the fabulous recipes in this book!

soups & starters

Historically, a formal banquet always included a substantial fish course before the meat was served. Today, with our ever-changing lifestyles and appetites, we are more likely to choose a light, elegant starter. Soup is always a good choice, and Breton Fish Soup is a chic, creamy French recipe, while Mexican Fish & Roasted Tomato Soup will get the tastebuds tingling and Thai Prawn & Scallop Soup is stylish, yet incredibly quick to make.

Spanish tapas have become popular in recent years – you need to serve a good selection, so there are delicious recipes for Fresh Salmon in Mojo Sauce, Cod & Caper Croquettes, Tuna with Pimiento-stuffed Olives, Mussels with Herb & Garlic Butter, Lime-drizzled Prawns and Calamari. Japanese sushi is another form of trendy starter – if you've never made it before, Teriyaki Tuna Pressed Sushi with French Bean Strips and Scattered Sushi with Prawns, Crab & Avocado are easy to assemble.

For those occasions when you're out to impress with classic simplicity, serve Salmon Tartare or Gravlax, two dishes where the fish is slowly 'seasoned' rather than cooked, Potted Crab, Prawn Cocktail or Blinis, a Russian speciality of buckwheat pancakes topped with soured cream and smoked salmon. Gorgeous!

breton fish soup

ingredients

SERVES 4

2 tsp butter
1 large leek, thinly sliced
2 shallots, finely chopped
125 ml/4 fl oz cider
300 ml/10 fl oz fish stock
250 g/9 oz potatoes, diced
1 bay leaf
salt
4 tbsp plain flour
200 ml/7 fl oz milk
200 ml/7 fl oz double cream
55 g/2 oz sorrel leaves
350 g/12 oz skinless
monkfish or cod fillets, cut
into 2.5-cm/1-inch pieces

method

1 Melt the butter in a large saucepan over a medium–low heat. Add the leek and shallots, and cook, stirring frequently, for 5 minutes, or until they start to soften. Add the cider and bring to the boil.

2 Stir in the stock, potatoes and bay leaf with a large pinch of salt (unless the stock is salty) and return to the boil. Reduce the heat, cover and cook gently for 10 minutes.

3 Put the flour in a small bowl and very slowly whisk in a few tablespoons of the milk to make a thick paste. Stir in a little more milk to make a smooth liquid.

4 Adjust the heat so that the soup bubbles gently. Stir in the flour mixture and cook, stirring frequently, for 5 minutes. Add the remaining milk and half the cream. Cook for a further 10 minutes, or until the potatoes are tender.

5 Finely chop the sorrel and combine with the remaining cream. Stir into the soup and add the fish. Cook, stirring occasionally, for a further 3 minutes, or until the monkfish stiffens or the cod just begins to flake. Taste the soup and adjust the seasoning, if necessary. Ladle into warmed bowls and serve.

mexican fish & roasted tomato soup

ingredients

SERVES 4

5 ripe tomatoes
5 garlic cloves, unpeeled
1 litre/1³/₄ pints fish stock
500 g/1 lb 2 oz red snapper fillets, cut into chunks
2–3 tbsp olive oil
1 onion, chopped
2 fresh chillies, deseeded and thinly sliced
lime wedges, to serve

method

1 Heat a dry, heavy-based frying pan over a high heat, add the tomatoes and garlic cloves, and cook, turning frequently, for 10–15 minutes until the skins are blackened and charred and the flesh is tender, or cook under a preheated hot grill. Alternatively, put the tomatoes and garlic cloves in a roasting tin and bake in a preheated oven at 190–200°C/375–400°F/ Gas Mark 5–6 for 40 minutes.

2 Let the tomatoes and garlic cool, then remove and discard the skins and roughly chop the flesh, combining it with any juices from the pan. Set aside.

3 Heat the stock in a saucepan over a medium heat until simmering, add the snapper and cook just until opaque and slightly firm. Remove from the heat and set aside.

4 Heat the oil in a separate saucepan, add the onion and cook, stirring frequently, for 5 minutes until softened. Strain in the fish cooking liquid, then add the tomatoes and garlic and stir well. Bring to the boil, then reduce the heat and simmer for 5 minutes to combine the flavours. Add the chillies.

5 Divide chunks of the poached fish between 4 soup bowls, ladle over the hot soup, and serve with lime wedges for squeezing over.

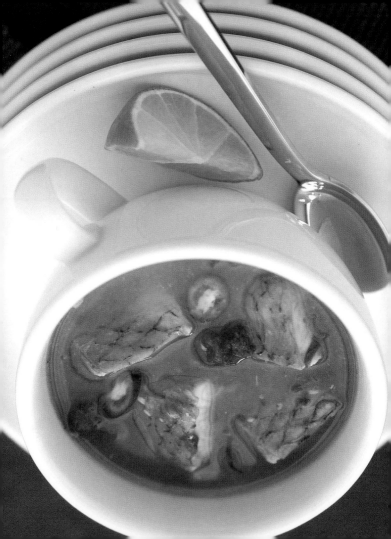

thai prawn & scallop soup

ingredients

SERVES 4

1 litre/1³/₄ pints fish stock

juice of ¹/₂ lime

2 tbsp rice wine or sherry

1 leek, sliced

2 shallots, finely chopped

1 tbsp grated fresh ginger

1 fresh red chilli, deseeded
and finely chopped

225 g/8 oz raw prawns,
peeled and deveined

225 g/8 oz live scallops,
shucked and cleaned

1¹/₂ tbsp chopped fresh
flat-leaf parsley, plus extra
to garnish

salt and pepper

method

1 Put the stock, lime juice, rice wine, leek, shallots, ginger and chilli in a large saucepan. Bring to the boil over a high heat, then reduce the heat, cover and simmer for 10 minutes.

2 Add the prawns, scallops and parsley, season with salt and pepper and cook for 1–2 minutes.

3 Remove the pan from the heat and ladle the soup into warmed serving bowls. Garnish with chopped parsley and serve.

crab & sweetcorn soup

ingredients

115 g/4 oz fresh or frozen crabmeat

600 ml/1 pint water

425 g/15 oz canned creamed sweetcorn, drained

1/2 tsp salt

pinch of pepper

2 tsp cornflour, dissolved in 2 tbsp water (optional)

1 egg, beaten

method

1 If using frozen crabmeat, blanch the flesh in boiling water for 30 seconds. Remove with a slotted spoon and set aside.

2 In a large saucepan, bring the water to the boil with the crab and sweetcorn and simmer for 2 minutes. Season with the salt and pepper. Stir in the cornflour, if using, and continue stirring until the soup has thickened. Rapidly stir in the egg and serve.

salmon tartare

ingredients

SERVES 4

500 g/1 lb 2 oz salmon fillet,
  skinned
2 tbsp sea salt
1 tbsp caster sugar
2 tbsp chopped fresh dill,
  plus extra sprigs to garnish
1 tbsp chopped fresh tarragon
1 tsp Dijon mustard
juice of 1 lemon
salt and pepper

topping

400 g/14 oz cream cheese
1 tbsp snipped fresh chives
pinch of paprika

method

1 Put the salmon in a shallow, non-metallic dish. Combine the sea salt, sugar and chopped dill in a small bowl, then rub the mixture into the fish until well coated. Season with pepper. Cover with clingfilm and chill in the refrigerator for at least 48 hours, turning the salmon once.

2 Put the tarragon in a bowl with the mustard, lemon juice, salt and pepper. Remove the salmon from the refrigerator, chop into small pieces and add to the bowl. Stir until the salmon is well coated.

3 To make the topping, put all the topping ingredients in a separate bowl and mix well together. Put a 10-cm/4-inch steel cooking ring or round biscuit cutter on each of 4 small serving plates. Divide the salmon between the 4 steel rings so that each ring is half full. Level the surface of each one, then top with the cream cheese mixture. Smooth the surfaces, then carefully remove the steel rings. Garnish with dill sprigs and serve.

gravlax

ingredients

SERVES 8–12

2 salmon fillets, with skin on,
about 450 g/1 lb each

6 tbsp roughly chopped
fresh dill

115 g/4 oz sea salt

50 g/1¾ oz sugar

1 tbsp white peppercorns,
roughly crushed

lemon slices and fresh dill
sprigs, to garnish

12 slices brown bread,
buttered, to serve

method

1 Rinse the salmon fillets under cold running water and dry with kitchen paper. Put 1 fillet, skin-side down, in a non-metallic dish.

2 Mix the dill, sea salt, sugar and peppercorns together in a small bowl. Spread this mixture over the fillet in the dish and put the second fillet, skin-side up, on top. Put a plate, the same size as the fish, on top and weigh down with 3–4 food cans.

3 Chill in the refrigerator for 2 days, turning the fish about every 12 hours and basting with any juices that come out of the fish.

4 Remove the salmon from the brine and thinly slice, without slicing the skin, as you would smoked salmon. Cut the buttered bread into triangles and serve with the salmon. Garnish with lemon slices and dill sprigs.

fresh salmon in mojo sauce

ingredients

SERVES 8

4 fresh salmon fillets,
    weighing about
    750 g/1 lb 10 oz in total
salt and pepper
3 tbsp olive oil
1 fresh flat-leaf parsley sprig,
    to garnish

mojo sauce

2 garlic cloves, peeled
2 tsp paprika
1 tsp ground cumin
5 tbsp extra virgin olive oil
2 tbsp white wine vinegar
salt

method

1 To prepare the mojo sauce, put the garlic, paprika and cumin in the bowl of a food processor and, using a pulsing action, blend for 1 minute to mix well together. With the motor still running, add 1 tablespoon of the olive oil, drop by drop, through the feeder tube. When it has been added, scrape down the sides of the bowl with a spatula, then very slowly continue to pour in the oil in a thin, steady stream, until all the oil has been added and the sauce has slightly thickened. Add the vinegar and blend for a further 1 minute. Season the sauce with salt.

2 To prepare the salmon, remove the skin, cut each fillet in half widthways, then cut lengthways into 2-cm/3/4-inch-thick slices, discarding any bones. Season the pieces of fish with salt and pepper.

3 Heat the olive oil in a large, heavy-based frying pan. When hot, add the pieces of fish and cook for about 10 minutes, depending on its thickness, turning occasionally until cooked and browned on both sides.

4 Transfer the salmon to a warmed serving dish, drizzle over some of the mojo sauce and serve hot, garnished with parsley, and accompanied by the remaining sauce.

salmon & prawn spring rolls with plum sauce

ingredients

SERVES 4

125 g/4^1/$_2$ oz salmon fillet,
  skinned, boned and cut
  into 3-mm/^{1}/$_8$-inch cubes
60 g/2^1/$_4$ oz beansprouts
60 g/2^1/$_4$ oz Chinese cabbage,
  finely shredded
25 g/1 oz spring onion, finely
  chopped
60 g/2^1/$_4$ oz red pepper,
  deseeded and finely sliced
  into strips
^{1}/$_4$ tsp five-spice powder
60 g/2^1/$_4$ oz cooked peeled
  prawns
4 spring roll wrappers, halved
  widthways
vegetable oil spray
^{1}/$_4$ tsp sesame seeds

plum sauce

100 ml/3^1/$_2$ fl oz water
50 ml/2 fl oz orange juice
^{1}/$_2$ tsp chopped red chilli
1 tsp grated fresh ginger
200 g/7 oz red plums, pitted
  weight
1 tsp chopped spring onion
1 tsp chopped fresh coriander
^{1}/$_4$ tsp sesame oil

method

1 To make the sauce, put the water, orange juice, chilli, ginger and plums into a saucepan and bring to the boil. Reduce the heat, cover and simmer for 10 minutes. Remove from the heat, blend with a hand-held electric blender, or use a food processor, then stir in the spring onion, coriander and sesame oil. Let cool.

2 Heat a non-stick wok over a high heat, add the salmon, and stir-fry for 1 minute. Remove from the wok with a slotted spoon onto a plate. Using the cooking juices from the salmon, stir-fry the vegetables with the five-spice powder until just tender, drain in a colander, then stir in the cooked salmon and prawns – the mixture should be quite dry to prevent the rolls from becoming soggy.

3 Divide the salmon and vegetable mixture into 8 portions. Spoon a portion along one short edge of each spring roll wrapper and roll up, tucking in the sides.

4 Lay the spring rolls on a non-stick baking sheet and spray lightly with vegetable oil, sprinkle with sesame seeds and bake in a preheated oven, 200°C/400°F/Gas Mark 6, for 12–15 minutes, or until golden brown. Serve the spring rolls, and hand round the cold plum sauce separately.

cod & caper croquettes

ingredients

MAKES 12

350 g/12 oz white fish fillets,
    such as cod, haddock or
    monkfish, skinned and
    boned
300 ml/10 fl oz milk
salt and pepper
4 tbsp olive oil or
    55 g/2 oz butter
55 g/2 oz plain flour
4 tbsp capers,
    roughly chopped
1 tsp paprika
1 garlic clove, crushed
1 tsp lemon juice
3 tbsp chopped fresh
    flat-leaf parsley, plus extra
    sprigs to garnish
1 egg, beaten
55 g/2 oz fresh white
    breadcrumbs
1 tbsp sesame seeds
corn oil, for deep-frying
lemon wedges, to garnish
mayonnaise, to serve

method

1 Put the fish fillets and milk in a large frying pan and season with salt and pepper. Bring to the boil, lower the heat and cook, covered, for 8–10 minutes, or until the fish flakes easily. Remove and flake the fish, reserving the milk.

2 Heat the olive oil in a saucepan. Stir in the flour to form a paste and cook gently, stirring, for 1 minute. Gradually stir in the reserved milk until smooth. Slowly bring to the boil, stirring, until the mixture thickens.

3 Remove from the heat, add the fish and beat until smooth. Add the capers, paprika, garlic, lemon juice and parsley, season again and mix well. Transfer to a dish, let cool, then chill, covered, for 2–3 hours.

4 Pour the beaten egg onto a plate. Combine the breadcrumbs and sesame seeds on another plate. Divide the fish mixture into 12 portions and form each into a 7.5-cm/3-inch sausage shape. Dip each croquette in the beaten egg, then coat it in the breadcrumb mixture. Chill for 1 hour.

5 Heat the oil in a deep pan to 180–190ºC/350–375ºF. Cook the croquettes, in batches, for 3 minutes, or until golden brown and crispy. Drain well on kitchen paper.

6 Serve piping hot, garnished with lemon wedges and parsley sprigs, and accompanied by a bowl of mayonnaise for dipping.

tuna with pimiento-stuffed olives

ingredients

SERVES 6

2 fresh tuna steaks, weighing
about 250 g/9 oz in total
and about 2.5 cm/1 inch
thick

5 tbsp olive oil

3 tbsp red wine vinegar

4 sprigs of fresh thyme,
plus extra to garnish

1 bay leaf

salt and pepper

2 tbsp plain flour

1 onion, finely chopped

2 garlic cloves, finely chopped

85 g/3 oz pimiento-stuffed
green olives, sliced

method

1 Remove the skin from the tuna steaks, then cut the steaks in half along the grain of the fish. Cut each half into 1-cm/1/2-inch-thick slices against the grain.

2 Put 3 tablespoons of the olive oil and the vinegar in a large, shallow, non-metallic dish. Strip the leaves from the sprigs of thyme, add these to the dish with the bay leaf, and season with salt and pepper. Add the prepared strips of tuna, cover the dish and marinate in the refrigerator overnight.

3 Put the flour in a plastic bag. Remove the tuna strips from the marinade, reserving the marinade for later, add them to the bag of flour and toss well until lightly coated.

4 Heat the remaining olive oil in a large frying pan. Add the onion and garlic and cook gently for 5–10 minutes, or until softened and golden brown. Add the tuna strips and cook for 2–5 minutes, turning several times, until the fish becomes opaque. Add the reserved marinade and olives and cook for a further 1–2 minutes, stirring, until the fish is tender and the sauce has thickened.

5 Serve the tuna and olives piping hot, garnished with thyme sprigs.

teriyaki tuna pressed sushi with french bean strips

ingredients

MAKES 15 PIECES

200 g/7 oz sushi-grade tuna
   or tuna fillet, thinly sliced

2 tbsp teriyaki sauce

1 tbsp oil

10 French beans, trimmed
   and cut in half

oil, for cooking

1 tsp toasted sesame seeds

2 tbsp Japanese mayonnaise

pickled ginger and wasabi
   paste, to serve

sushi rice

125 g/4^1/$_2$ oz sushi rice,
   washed under cold
   running water until the
   water runs clear, then
   drained

160 ml/5^1/$_2$ fl oz water

^{1}/$_2$ piece of kombu

1 tbsp sushi rice seasoning

method

1 Put the sushi rice in a saucepan with the water and kombu, cover and bring rapidly to the boil. Remove the kombu, then re-cover, reduce the heat and simmer for 10 minutes. Turn off the heat and let the rice stand, covered, for 15 minutes. Put the hot rice in a large, very shallow bowl, pour the seasoning evenly over the surface, and mix it carefully into the rice with a spatula, using quick cutting strokes. Fan the rice with your hand to cool it.

2 Coat the tuna slices in the teriyaki sauce and cook in the oil in a frying pan for 1 minute on each side, then cut into thick strips. Blanch the French beans in boiling water for a minute, then cool under cold running water and drain.

3 Oil an 18-cm/7-inch loose-based square cake tin and line it with a piece of clingfilm large enough to hang over the edges. Oil the clingfilm and sprinkle in the sesame seeds. Pack the rice into the tin, spread over the mayonnaise, then arrange the tuna and beans in thick, diagonal strips. Cover with clingfilm, then put another tin on top and weigh down.

4 Chill for 15 minutes, then loosen the sides of the tin, and pull out the sushi. Cut into 15 pieces with a wet, sharp knife. Serve with pickled ginger and wasabi paste.

scattered sushi with prawns, crab & avocado

ingredients

SERVES 4

6 large raw prawns, peeled
    and deveined, tails left on

1 tbsp oil

1 cooked prepared crab

1 double quantity freshly
    cooked sushi rice
    (see page 28)

juice and grated rind of
    1 lemon

1 ripe avocado, cut into strips

1/2 cucumber, peeled and cut
    into slices

method

1 Sauté the prawns for 2 minutes on each side in the oil. Once they are cooked, set aside to cool. Lift the crabmeat out of the shell.

2 Mix the sushi rice with the lemon juice and grated lemon rind.

3 Divide the rice between 4 wooden or ceramic bowls. Arrange the prawns, crab, avocado and cucumber on top of the rice.

mussels with herb & garlic butter

ingredients

SERVES 8

800 g/1 lb 12 oz fresh mussels, in their shells

splash of dry white wine

1 bay leaf

85 g/3 oz butter

350 g/12 oz fresh white or brown breadcrumbs

4 tbsp chopped fresh flat-leaf parsley, plus extra sprigs to garnish

2 tbsp snipped fresh chives

2 garlic cloves, finely chopped

salt and pepper

lemon wedges, to serve

method

1 To prepare the mussels, scrub the shells under cold running water and pull off any beards. Discard any with broken shells. Tap the remaining mussels and discard any that refuse to close.

2 Put the mussels in a large saucepan and add the wine and the bay leaf. Cook, covered, over a high heat for 5 minutes, shaking the pan occasionally, or until the mussels are opened. Drain the mussels and discard any that remain closed. Shell the mussels, reserving one half of each shell. Arrange the mussels, in their half shells, in a large, shallow, ovenproof serving dish.

3 Melt the butter and pour into a small bowl. Add the breadcrumbs, parsley, chives, garlic, salt and pepper and mix well together. Let stand until the butter has set slightly. Using your fingers or 2 teaspoons, take a large pinch of the herb and butter mixture and use to fill each mussel shell, pressing it down well.

4 To serve, bake the mussels in a preheated oven, 230°C/450°F/Gas Mark 8, for 10 minutes, or until hot. Serve immediately, garnished with parsley sprigs, and accompanied by lemon wedges for squeezing over them.

potted crab

ingredients

SERVES 4–6

1 large cooked crab, prepared
    if possible

salt and pepper

whole nutmeg, for grating

2 pinches of cayenne pepper

juice of 1 lemon, or to taste

225 g/8 oz lightly salted butter

buttered toast slices and
    lemon wedges, to serve

method

1 If the crab is not already prepared, pick out all the white and brown meat, taking great care to remove all the meat from the claws.

2 Mix the white and brown meat together in a bowl, but do not mash too smoothly. Season well with salt and pepper and add a good grating of nutmeg, the cayenne pepper and the lemon juice.

3 Melt half the butter in a saucepan over a medium heat and carefully stir in the crabmeat. Turn the mixture out into 4–6 small soufflé dishes or ramekins.

4 Melt the remaining butter in a clean saucepan over a medium heat, then continue heating for a few moments until it stops bubbling. Allow the sediment to settle, then carefully pour the clarified butter over the crab mixture. Cover and chill in the refrigerator for at least 1 hour before serving with buttered toast and lemon wedges. The seal of clarified butter allows the potted crab to be kept for 1–2 days.

prawn cocktail

ingredients

SERVES 4

$1/2$ iceberg lettuce, finely
    shredded
150 ml/5 fl oz mayonnaise
2 tbsp single cream
2 tbsp tomato ketchup
few drops of Tabasco sauce,
    or to taste
juice of $1/2$ lemon, or to taste
salt and pepper
175 g/6 oz cooked peeled
    prawns
paprika, for sprinkling
4 cooked prawns, in their
    shells, and 4 lemon slices,
    to garnish
thin buttered brown bread
    slices (optional), to serve

method

1 Divide the lettuce between 4 small serving dishes (traditionally, stemmed glass ones, but any small dishes will be fine).

2 Mix the mayonnaise, cream and tomato ketchup together in a bowl. Add the Tabasco sauce and lemon juice and season well with salt and pepper.

3 Divide the peeled prawns equally between the dishes and pour over the dressing. Cover and chill in the refrigerator for 30 minutes.

4 Sprinkle a little paprika over the cocktails and garnish each dish with a prawn and a lemon slice. Serve the cocktails with slices of brown bread and butter.

lime-drizzled prawns

ingredients

SERVES 6

4 limes

12 raw jumbo prawns,
    in their shells

3 tbsp olive oil

2 garlic cloves, finely chopped

splash of fino sherry

salt and pepper

4 tbsp chopped fresh
    flat-leaf parsley

method

1 Grate the rind and squeeze the juice from 2 of the limes. Cut the remaining 2 limes into wedges and set aside for later.

2 To prepare the prawns, remove the head and legs, leaving the shells and tails intact. Using a sharp knife, make a shallow slit along the back of each prawn, then pull out the dark vein and discard. Rinse the prawns under cold water and dry on kitchen paper.

3 Heat the olive oil in a large, heavy-based frying pan, then add the garlic and cook for 30 seconds. Add the prawns and cook for 5 minutes, stirring from time to time, or until they turn pink and start to curl. Mix in the lime rind and juice and a splash of sherry to moisten, then stir well together.

4 Transfer the cooked prawns to a serving dish, season with salt and pepper and sprinkle with the parsley. Serve piping hot, accompanied by the reserved lime wedges for squeezing over the prawns.

calamari

ingredients

SERVES 6

450 g/1 lb prepared squid

plain flour, for coating

sunflower oil, for deep-frying

salt

lemon wedges, to garnish

garlic mayonnaise, to serve

method

1 Slice the squid into 1-cm/^{1}/$_2$-inch rings and halve the tentacles if large. Rinse under cold running water and dry well with kitchen paper. Dust the squid rings with flour so that they are lightly coated.

2 Heat the oil in a deep pan to 180–190ºC/ 350–375ºF, or until a cube of bread browns in 30 seconds. Deep-fry the squid rings in small batches for 2–3 minutes, or until golden brown and crisp all over, turning several times (if you deep-fry too many squid rings at one time, the oil temperature will drop and they will be soggy). Do not overcook as the squid will become tough and rubbery rather than moist and tender.

3 Remove with a slotted spoon and drain well on kitchen paper. Keep warm in a low oven while you deep-fry the remaining squid rings.

4 Sprinkle the fried squid rings with salt and serve piping hot, garnished with lemon wedges for squeezing over. Accompany with a bowl of garlic mayonnaise for dipping.

blinis

ingredients

MAKES 8

115 g/4 oz buckwheat flour
115 g/4 oz white bread flour
7-g/¼-oz sachet easy-blend
    dried yeast
1 tsp salt
400 ml/14 fl oz tepid milk
2 eggs, 1 whole and
    1 separated
vegetable oil, for brushing
soured cream and smoked
    salmon, to serve

method

1 Sift both flours into a large, warmed bowl. Stir in the yeast and salt. Beat in the milk, whole egg and egg yolk until smooth. Cover the bowl and let stand in a warm place for 1 hour.

2 Place the egg white in a spotlessly clean bowl and whisk until soft peaks form. Fold into the batter. Brush a heavy-based frying pan with oil and set over a medium–high heat. When the pan is hot, pour enough of the batter onto the surface to make a blini about the size of a saucer.

3 When bubbles rise, turn the blini over with a spatula and cook the other side until light brown. Wrap in a clean tea towel to keep warm while cooking the remainder. Serve the warm blinis with soured cream and smoked salmon.

lunch & supper dishes

Fish is just made for lunch and supper dishes. It is light and easily digestible, so you won't find yourself needing to sleep off your lunch or be unable to sleep after supper. It works brilliantly in all sorts of dishes, from thick, delicious chowders to elegant tarts – for speed, try Smoked Salmon, Red Onion & Goat's Cheese Tarts or Smoked Salmon, Feta & Dill Filo Parcels, and if you have a little more time to spare, Smoked Fish & Gruyère Soufflé Tart melts in the mouth and tastes out of this world.

Fish marries well with eggs – try Scrambled Eggs with Smoked Salmon, the perfect brunch dish, a really satisfying Salmon Frittata, or Chinese fast food in the form of Prawn Fu Yung. It is also a favourite ingredient in Mexican snacks, such as Fish Tacos Ensenada-style and Fish Burritos.

Fish Cakes and Smoked Fish Pie are great for family meals, needing only a watercress salad or lightly cooked vegetables to accompany. For lunch or supper parties, Seafood in a Light Broth with Vegetables is a very attractive French dish, Potato, Herb & Smoked Salmon Gratin and Scallops in Saffron Sauce are definitely out of the ordinary, and soufflés never fail to draw a gasp of admiration from your guests. The Crab Soufflé will definitely do that!

scrambled eggs with smoked salmon

ingredients

SERVES 4

8 eggs

6 tbsp single cream

2 tbsp chopped fresh dill,
    plus extra to garnish

salt and pepper

100 g/3^1/$_2$ oz smoked salmon,
    cut into small pieces

2 tbsp butter

slices rustic bread, toasted

method

1 Break the eggs into a large bowl and whisk together with the cream and dill. Season with salt and pepper. Add the smoked salmon and mix to combine.

2 Melt the butter in a large non-stick frying pan and pour in the egg and smoked salmon mixture. Using a wooden spatula, gently scrape the egg away from the sides of the frying pan as it starts to set and swirl the frying pan slightly to allow the uncooked egg to fill the surface.

3 When the eggs are almost cooked but still creamy, remove from the heat and spoon onto the prepared toast. Serve immediately, garnished with sprigs of dill.

salmon frittata

ingredients

SERVES 6

250 g/9 oz skinless, boneless
   salmon

3 fresh thyme sprigs

1 fresh parsley sprig, plus
   2 tbsp chopped fresh
   parsley

5 black peppercorns

1/2 small onion, sliced

1/2 celery stick, sliced

1/2 carrot, chopped

175 g/6 oz asparagus spears,
   chopped

85 g/3 oz baby carrots, halved

3 1/2 tbsp butter

1 large onion, finely sliced

1 garlic clove, finely chopped

115 g/4 oz fresh or frozen
   peas

8 eggs, lightly beaten

1 tbsp chopped fresh dill

salt and pepper

lemon wedges, to garnish

soured cream, salad and
   crusty bread, to serve

method

1 Put the salmon in a saucepan with 1 thyme sprig, the parsley sprig, peppercorns, onion, celery and carrot. Cover with cold water and bring slowly to the boil. Remove the pan from the heat and let stand for 5 minutes. Remove the fish with a slotted spoon, flake and set aside. Discard the vegetables and cooking liquid.

2 Bring a large saucepan of salted water to the boil and blanch the asparagus for 2 minutes. Drain and refresh under cold running water. Blanch the baby carrots for 4 minutes. Drain and refresh under cold running water. Drain both again, pat dry and set aside.

3 Heat half the butter in a large ovenproof frying pan over a low–medium heat, add the onion and cook, stirring, until softened. Add the garlic and remaining thyme and cook, stirring, for 1 minute. Add the asparagus, carrots and peas and heat through.

4 Transfer to the eggs in a bowl with the chopped parsley, dill and salmon. Season and stir briefly. Heat the remaining butter in the pan over a low heat and return the mixture to the pan. Cover and cook for 10 minutes.

5 Cook under a preheated medium grill for a further 5 minutes until set and golden. Serve hot or cold in wedges, topped with a spoonful of soured cream, with salad and crusty bread. Garnish with lemon wedges.

fluffy prawn omelette

ingredients

SERVES 2-4

115 g/4 oz cooked peeled
    prawns, thawed if frozen

4 spring onions, chopped

55 g/2 oz courgette, grated

4 eggs, separated

few dashes of Tabasco sauce,
    to taste

3 tbsp milk

salt and pepper

1 tbsp corn or olive oil

25 g/1 oz mature Cheddar
    cheese, grated

method

1 Pat the prawns dry with kitchen paper, then mix with the spring onions and courgette in a bowl and set aside.

2 Using a fork, beat the egg yolks with the Tabasco, milk, salt and pepper in a separate bowl.

3 Whisk the egg whites in a large bowl until stiff, then gently stir the egg yolk mixture into the egg whites, taking care not to overmix.

4 Heat the oil in a large, non-stick frying pan and when hot pour in the egg mixture. Cook over a low heat for 4–6 minutes, or until lightly set. Preheat the grill.

5 Spoon the prawn mixture on top of the eggs and sprinkle with the cheese. Cook under the preheated grill for 2–3 minutes, or until set and the top is golden brown. Cut into wedges and serve immediately.

prawn fu yung

ingredients

SERVES 4–6

1 tbsp vegetable or peanut oil

115 g/4 oz raw prawns,
    peeled and deveined

4 eggs, lightly beaten

1 tsp salt

pinch of white pepper

2 tbsp finely chopped
    Chinese chives

method

1 In a preheated wok or frying pan, heat the vegetable or peanut oil and stir-fry the prawns until they begin to turn pink.

2 Season the beaten eggs with the salt and pepper and pour over the prawns. Stir-fry for 1 minute, then add the chives.

3 Cook for a further 4 minutes, stirring all the time, until the eggs are cooked through but still soft in texture, and serve immediately.

crab soufflé

ingredients

SERVES 4–6

3 tbsp butter, plus extra
    for greasing
25 g/1 oz dried breadcrumbs
1 small onion, finely chopped
1 garlic clove, crushed
2 tsp mustard powder
25 g/1 oz plain flour
225 ml/8 fl oz milk
50 g/1³⁄₄ oz Gruyère cheese,
    grated
3 eggs, separated
225 g/8 oz fresh crabmeat,
    thawed if frozen
2 tbsp snipped fresh chives
pinch of cayenne pepper
salt and pepper

method

1 Generously grease a 1.5-litre/2³⁄₄-pint soufflé dish. Add the breadcrumbs and shake around the dish to coat completely, shaking out any excess. Set aside on a baking sheet.

2 Melt the butter in a large saucepan over a low heat, add the onion and cook, stirring occasionally, for 8 minutes, until softened but not browned. Add the garlic and cook, stirring, for 1 minute. Then add the mustard powder and flour and continue stirring for another minute. Gradually add the milk, stirring constantly, until smooth. Increase the heat slightly and bring slowly to the boil, stirring constantly. Simmer gently for 2 minutes. Remove from the heat and stir in the cheese. Let cool slightly.

3 Lightly beat in the egg yolks, then fold in the crabmeat, chives, cayenne, salt and pepper.

4 Whisk the egg whites in a large, clean, greasefree bowl until they hold stiff peaks. Add a large spoonful of the egg whites to the crab mixture and fold together to slacken. Add the remaining egg whites and fold together carefully but thoroughly. Spoon into the prepared dish.

5 Cook in a preheated oven, 200°C/400°F/ Gas Mark 6, for 25 minutes until well risen and golden. Serve immediately.

seafood in a light broth with vegetables

ingredients

SERVES 4

small pinch of saffron threads
55 g/2 oz unsalted butter
2 carrots, peeled and cut into
    julienne strips
2 celery sticks, cut into
    julienne strips
1 courgette, cut into julienne
    strips
1 shallot, very finely chopped
2 garlic cloves, very finely
    chopped
1 bouquet garni
salt and pepper
200 ml/7 fl oz dry white wine
200 ml/7 fl oz water
8 pieces of mixed fresh fish,
    such as salmon fillets and
    monkfish medallions, or
    only 1 type of fish, all skin
    and bones removed, each
    piece about 125 g/4½ oz
250 ml/9 fl oz soured cream
fresh chervil sprigs, to garnish

method

1 Put the saffron threads in a small dry frying pan over a high heat and toast, stirring, for 1 minute, or until you can smell the aroma. Immediately tip out of the pan and set aside.

2 Melt the butter over a medium heat in a frying pan with a tight-fitting lid. Add the carrots, celery, courgette, shallot, garlic, bouquet garni, salt and pepper. Sauté for 3 minutes, without letting the vegetables colour.

3 Meanwhile, bring the wine and water to the boil in a saucepan over a high heat, then boil for 2 minutes. Pour the boiling liquid over the vegetables, then reduce the heat to low and simmer for 5 minutes. Remove from the heat and discard the bouquet garni.

4 Place the fish over the vegetables in a single layer, then cover and simmer for 5 minutes, or until the fish is cooked through and flakes easily. Remove the fish and vegetables to a warmed bowl and spoon over a little of the poaching liquid. Cover with foil and set aside.

5 Stir the soured cream and saffron into the poaching liquid and bring to the boil, stirring. Boil for 3–5 minutes to reduce. Place a mound of vegetables on each soup plate and top with the fish. Spoon over the reduced liquid and garnish with the chervil.

smoked fish chowder

ingredients

SERVES 4

2 tbsp butter

1 onion, finely chopped

1 small celery stick, finely diced

250 g/9 oz potatoes, diced

55 g/2 oz carrots, diced

300 ml/10 fl oz boiling water

salt and pepper

350 g/12 oz smoked cod
    fillets, skinned and cut
    into bite-sized pieces

300 ml/10 fl oz milk

method

1 Melt the butter in a large saucepan over a low heat, add the onion and celery and cook, stirring frequently, for 5 minutes, or until softened but not browned.

2 Add the potatoes, carrots, water, salt and pepper. Bring to the boil, then reduce the heat and simmer for 10 minutes, or until the vegetables are tender. Add the fish to the chowder and cook for a further 10 minutes.

3 Pour in the milk and heat gently. Taste and adjust the seasoning, if necessary. Serve hot.

potato, herb & smoked salmon gratin

ingredients

SERVES 6

400 ml/14 fl oz milk

3 whole cloves

2 bay leaves

50 g/1³/4 oz onion, sliced

85 g/3 oz leek, chopped

100 g/3¹/2 oz lightly cured
    smoked salmon, finely
    sliced into strips

350 g/12 oz potatoes, cut into
    2-mm/¹/16-inch slices

2 tbsp finely chopped
    fresh chives

2 tbsp finely chopped
    fresh dill

1 tbsp finely chopped fresh
    tarragon

2 tsp wholegrain mustard

oil, for greasing

pepper

sprigs of watercress, to
    garnish

method

1 Pour the milk into a large, heavy-based saucepan, add the cloves, bay leaves, onion, leek and smoked salmon and heat over a low heat. When the milk is just about to reach simmering point, carefully remove the smoked salmon with a slotted spoon and cool on a plate.

2 Add the potatoes to the milk and stir with a wooden spoon. Return to a simmer and cook, stirring occasionally to prevent the potatoes from sticking, for 12 minutes, or until the potatoes are just beginning to soften and the milk has thickened slightly from the potato starch. Remove the cloves and bay leaves.

3 Add the herbs, mustard and pepper and stir well. Pour the mixture into a greased and base-lined 19-cm/7¹/2-inch shallow cake tin. Cover with a layer of greaseproof paper and then foil and bake in a preheated oven, 200°C/400°F/Gas Mark 6, for 30 minutes.

4 Remove from the oven and place a tin on top. Leave to cool for 20 minutes before turning out onto a baking sheet. Put under a preheated hot grill to brown the top.

5 Cut the gratin into 6 wedges and serve with the smoked salmon, garnished with sprigs of watercress.

grilled tuna
& vegetable kebabs

ingredients

SERVES 4

4 tuna steaks, about 140 g/
    5 oz each
2 red onions
12 cherry tomatoes
1 red pepper, deseeded and
    diced into 2.5-cm/1-inch
    pieces
1 yellow pepper, deseeded
    and diced into 2.5-cm/
    1-inch pieces
1 courgette, sliced
1 tbsp chopped fresh oregano
4 tbsp olive oil
pepper
lime wedges, to garnish
selection of salads and
    cooked couscous, new
    potatoes or bread,
    to serve

method

1 Cut the tuna into 2.5-cm/1-inch dice. Peel the onions, leaving the root intact, and cut each onion lengthways into 6 wedges.

2 Divide the fish and vegetables evenly between 8 wooden skewers (presoaked to avoid burning) and arrange on the grill pan.

3 Mix the oregano and oil together in a small bowl. Season with pepper. Lightly brush the kebabs with the oil and cook under a grill preheated to high for 10–15 minutes or until evenly cooked, turning occasionally. If you cannot fit all the kebabs on the grill pan at once, cook them in batches, keeping the cooked kebabs warm while cooking the remainder. Alternatively, these kebabs can be cooked on a barbecue.

4 Garnish with lime wedges and serve with a selection of salads and cooked couscous, new potatoes or bread.

garlic & herb prawns

ingredients

SERVES 2

12 raw jumbo prawns, in
     their shells
juice of $1/2$ lemon
2 garlic cloves, crushed
3 tbsp chopped fresh parsley
1 tbsp chopped fresh dill
3 tbsp softened butter
salt and pepper

to serve

lemon wedges
crusty bread
salad

method

1 Rinse and peel the prawns. Devein, using a sharp knife to slice along the back from the head end to the tail, and removing the thin black intestine.

2 Mix the lemon juice with the garlic, herbs and butter to form a paste. Season well with salt and pepper. Spread the paste over the prawns and marinate for 30 minutes.

3 Cook the prawns under a preheated medium grill for 5–6 minutes. Alternatively, heat a frying pan and fry the prawns in the paste until cooked. Turn out onto hot plates and pour over the juices. Serve immediately with lemon wedges, some crusty bread and salad.

scallops in saffron sauce

ingredients

SERVES 8

150 ml/5 fl oz dry white wine
150 ml/5 fl oz fish stock
large pinch of saffron threads
900 g/2 lb shucked scallops,
    preferably large ones,
    with corals
salt and pepper
3 tbsp olive oil
1 small onion, finely chopped
2 garlic cloves, finely chopped
150 ml/5 fl oz double cream
squeeze of lemon juice
chopped fresh flat-leaf
    parsley, to garnish
crusty bread, to serve

method

1 Put the wine, fish stock and saffron in a saucepan and bring to the boil. Lower the heat, cover and simmer gently for 15 minutes.

2 Meanwhile, remove and discard from each scallop the tough, white muscle that is found opposite the coral, and separate the coral from the scallop. Slice the scallops and corals vertically into thick slices. Dry well on kitchen paper, then season with salt and pepper.

3 Heat the olive oil in a large, heavy-based frying pan. Add the onion and garlic and cook until softened and lightly browned. Add the sliced scallops to the pan and cook gently for 5 minutes, stirring occasionally, or until they turn just opaque. Overcooking the scallops will make them tough and rubbery.

4 Using a slotted spoon, remove the scallops from the frying pan and transfer to a warmed plate. Add the saffron liquid to the pan, bring to the boil and boil rapidly until reduced by about half. Lower the heat and gradually stir in the cream, just a little at a time. Simmer gently until the sauce thickens.

5 Return the scallops to the pan and simmer for 1–2 minutes just to heat through. Add a squeeze of lemon juice and season with salt and pepper. Serve the scallops hot, garnished with the parsley, with slices or chunks of crusty bread.

fish cakes

ingredients

SERVES 4

450 g/1 lb floury potatoes,
　　such as King Edward or
　　Estima, peeled and cut
　　into chunks
450 g/1 lb mixed fish fillets,
　　such as cod and salmon,
　　skinned
2 tbsp chopped fresh tarragon
grated rind of 1 lemon
2 tbsp double cream
salt and pepper
1 tbsp plain flour
1 egg, beaten
115 g/4 oz breadcrumbs,
　　made from day-old white
　　or wholewheat bread
4 tbsp vegetable oil
lemon wedges, to garnish
watercress salad, to serve

method

1 Bring a large saucepan of salted water to the boil, add the potatoes and cook for 15–20 minutes. Drain well, then mash with a potato masher or fork until smooth.

2 Put the fish in a frying pan and just cover with water. Bring to the boil over a medium heat, then reduce the heat to low, cover and simmer gently for 5 minutes until cooked. Remove with a slotted spoon and drain on a plate. When cool enough to handle, flake the fish roughly into good-sized pieces, removing and discarding any bones.

3 Mix the mashed potatoes with the fish, tarragon, lemon rind and cream in a bowl. Season well with salt and pepper and shape into 4 round cakes or 8 smaller ones.

4 Put the flour, egg and breadcrumbs in separate bowls. Dust the fish cakes with flour, dip into the beaten egg, then coat thoroughly in the breadcrumbs. Put on a baking sheet, cover and chill in the refrigerator for at least 30 minutes.

5 Heat the oil in the frying pan over a medium heat, add the fish cakes and cook for 5 minutes on each side, turning them with a spatula. Serve hot, garnished with lemon wedges, with a watercress salad to accompany.

fish tacos ensenada-style

ingredients

SERVES 4

450 g/1 lb firm-fleshed white
   fish, such as red snapper
   or cod
1/4 tsp dried oregano
1/4 tsp ground cumin
1 tsp mild chilli powder
2–3 garlic cloves, finely
   chopped
salt and pepper
3 tbsp plain flour
vegetable oil, for frying
1/4 red cabbage, thinly sliced
   or shredded
juice of 2 limes
hot pepper sauce or salsa
   to taste
8 soft corn tortillas
1 tbsp chopped fresh
   coriander
1/2 onion, chopped (optional)
salsa of your choice

method

1 Place the fish on a plate and sprinkle with half the oregano, cumin, chilli powder, garlic, and salt and pepper, then dust with the flour.

2 Heat the oil in a frying pan until it is smoking, then fry the fish in several batches until it is golden on the outside and just tender in the middle. Remove from the pan and place on kitchen paper to drain.

3 Combine the cabbage with the remaining oregano, cumin, chilli and garlic, then stir in the lime juice, and season with salt and hot pepper sauce. Set aside.

4 Heat the tortillas in an ungreased non-stick frying pan, sprinkling with a few drops of water as they heat; wrap the tortillas in a clean tea towel as you work to keep them warm. Alternatively, heat through in a stack in the pan, alternating the top and bottom tortillas so that they warm evenly.

5 Place some of the warm fried fish in each tortilla, along with a big spoonful of the cabbage salad. Sprinkle with fresh coriander and onion, if using. Add salsa to taste and serve immediately.

fish burritos

ingredients

SERVES 4–6

about 450 g/1 lb firm-fleshed
    white fish fillets, such as
    red snapper or cod, skinned
salt and pepper
1/4 tsp ground cumin
pinch of dried oregano
4 garlic cloves, finely chopped
125 ml/4 fl oz fish stock
juice of 1/2 lemon or lime
8 flour tortillas
2–3 romaine lettuce leaves,
    shredded
2 ripe tomatoes, diced
salsa of your choice
lemon wedges, to garnish

method

1 Season the fish with salt and pepper, then put in a saucepan with the cumin, oregano, garlic and enough stock to cover.

2 Bring to the boil and boil for 1 minute. Remove the saucepan from the heat and let the fish cool in the cooking liquid for about 30 minutes.

3 Remove the fish with a slotted spoon. Flake the fish into bite-sized pieces and put in a non-metallic bowl. Sprinkle with the lemon juice and set aside.

4 Heat the tortillas in a dry non-stick frying pan over a medium heat, sprinkling with a few drops of water as they heat; wrap in a clean tea towel as you work to keep them warm. Alternatively, heat through in a stack in the pan, alternating the tortillas from the top to the bottom to warm evenly.

5 Arrange some lettuce in the centre of 1 tortilla, spoon on a few fish chunks, then sprinkle with a little tomato. Top with some salsa. Repeat with the other tortillas and serve immediately, garnished with lemon wedges.

smoked fish pie

ingredients

SERVES 6

675 g/1 lb 8 oz potatoes,
    unpeeled
2 tbsp olive oil
1 onion, finely chopped
1 leek, thinly sliced
1 carrot, diced
1 celery stick, diced
115 g/4 oz mushrooms, halved
grated rind of 1 lemon
350 g/12 oz skinless,
    boneless smoked cod or
    haddock fillet, cubed
350 g/12 oz skinless,
    boneless white fish, cubed
8 oz/225 g cooked
    peeled prawns
2 tbsp chopped fresh parsley
1 tbsp chopped fresh dill,
    plus sprigs to garnish
salt and pepper
4 tbsp butter, melted
25 g/1 oz Gruyère
    cheese, grated
cooked vegetables, to serve

sauce

4 tbsp butter
4 tbsp plain flour
1 tsp mustard powder
600 ml/1 pint milk
85 g/3 oz Gruyère
    cheese, grated

method

1 For the sauce, melt the butter in a large saucepan, add the flour and mustard powder and stir until smooth. Cook over a very low heat for 2 minutes. Slowly beat in the milk, while heating, until smooth. Simmer gently for 2 minutes then stir in the cheese until smooth. Remove from the heat and cover the surface of the sauce with clingfilm. Set aside.

2 Meanwhile, boil the whole potatoes in plenty of salted water for 15 minutes. Drain well and set aside until cool enough to handle.

3 Heat the oil in a clean saucepan. Add the onion and cook for 5 minutes until softened. Add the leek, carrot, celery and mushrooms and cook for a further 10 minutes, or until the vegetables have softened. Stir in the lemon rind and cook briefly. Add the vegetables to the sauce with the fish, prawns, parsley and dill. Season and transfer to a greased 1.7-litre/ 3-pint casserole dish.

4 Peel the cooled potatoes and grate them roughly. Mix with the melted butter. Cover the filling with the potato and sprinkle with the cheese. Cover loosely with foil and bake in a preheated oven, 200°C/400°F/Gas Mark 6, for 30 minutes. Remove the foil and bake for a further 30 minutes, or until the topping is golden and the filling is bubbling. Garnish with dill sprigs and serve with vegetables.

smoked fish & gruyère soufflé tart

ingredients

SERVES 6

pastry

125 g/4¹/₂ oz plain flour, plus
    extra for dusting

pinch of salt

¹/₂ tsp English mustard
    powder

4 tbsp cold butter, diced, plus
    extra for greasing

1 egg yolk, mixed with a little
    cold water

filling

300 ml/10 fl oz milk

1 bay leaf

250 g/9 oz skinless, boneless,
    undyed smoked fish

2 tbsp butter

25 g/1 oz plain flour

¹/₂ tsp ground nutmeg

white pepper

125 g/4¹/₂ oz Gruyère cheese,
    grated

2 eggs, separated

method

1 Sift the flour, salt and mustard into a food processor, add the butter and process to resemble breadcrumbs. Add the egg yolk and pulse to bring the dough together. Roll out the dough on a lightly floured work surface and use to line a greased 23-cm/9-inch loose-based fluted tart tin. Trim the edge, line the tart shell with baking paper and fill with dried beans. Chill for 30 minutes, then bake in a preheated oven, 190°C/375°F/Gas Mark 5, for 10 minutes. Remove the paper and beans, bake for a further 5 minutes, then remove from the oven. Increase the temperature to 200°C/400°F/Gas Mark 6.

2 Bring the milk and bay leaf to a simmer in a frying pan, add the fish and cook for 3–5 minutes until just cooked. Remove the fish with a slotted spoon, reserving the milk but discarding the bay leaf. Cool then flake the fish.

3 Melt the butter in a saucepan, stir in the flour and cook, stirring, for 2–3 minutes. Slowly add the reserved milk and cook, stirring, until thickened. Stir in the nutmeg and pepper, then the cheese. Remove from the heat, stir in the egg yolks and fish, and cool slightly. Whisk the egg whites in a clean bowl until stiff, then fold quickly into the fish mixture. Pour into the tart shell and bake for 15 minutes until risen and browned. Let rest for 10 minutes, then serve.

smoked cod & prawn tart

ingredients

SERVES 4–6

pastry

200 g/7 oz plain flour

large pinch of salt

100 g/3¹/₂ oz margarine, diced, plus extra for greasing

1 egg yolk

3 tbsp ice-cold water

filling

400 g/14 oz undyed smoked cod fillet, rinsed and dried

300 ml/10 fl oz milk

150 g/5¹/₂ oz cooked peeled prawns

200 g/7 oz cream cheese

3 eggs, beaten

3 tbsp snipped fresh chives

pepper

method

1 To make the pastry, sift the flour and salt into a mixing bowl, then rub in the margarine until the mixture resembles coarse breadcrumbs. Stir in the egg yolk, followed by the water, then bring the mixture together into a ball. Turn out on to a lightly floured work surface and knead until smooth. Wrap in clingfilm and chill in the refrigerator for 30 minutes.

2 Meanwhile, put the fish into a shallow saucepan with the milk. Heat gently until simmering and simmer for 10 minutes, or until just cooked and opaque. Remove the fish with a slotted spoon, cool a little, then peel away the skin and discard any bones. Flake the fish into large chunks and set aside. Reserve 125 ml/4 fl oz of the cooking liquid.

3 Roll out the dough and use to line a lightly greased 26-cm/10¹/₂-inch tart tin. Line the tart shell with baking paper and dried beans and bake in a preheated oven, 200°C/400°F/ Gas Mark 6, for 8 minutes. Remove the paper and beans and bake for 5 minutes more.

4 Arrange the fish and prawns in the tart shell. Beat the cream cheese, reserved cooking liquid, eggs, chives and pepper in a bowl, then pour over the seafood. Bake for 30 minutes, or until set and golden brown.

smoked salmon, red onion & goat's cheese tarts

ingredients

SERVES 4

250 g/9 oz good-quality puff
    pastry

plain flour, for rolling

1 egg, lightly beaten with
    1 tbsp milk

1 small red onion, sliced

100 g/3½ oz goat's cheese,
    crumbled

4 slices smoked salmon

pepper

method

1 Roll the puff pastry out to 5 mm/¼ inch thick on a lightly floured work surface and cut into 4 even-size squares. Place on an ungreased baking sheet and brush each square lightly with the egg mixture. Divide the sliced onion evenly between the tarts and top with goat's cheese.

2 Bake in a preheated oven, 200°C/400°F/Gas Mark 6, for 20–25 minutes, or until the pastry has risen and is golden brown. Cool slightly, then top with the slices of smoked salmon and season with pepper. Serve immediately.

smoked salmon, feta & dill filo parcels

ingredients

MAKES 6 PARCELS

150 g/5¹/2 oz feta cheese, crumbled

250 g/9 oz ricotta cheese

150 g/5¹/2 oz smoked salmon, diced

2 tbsp chopped fresh dill

2 tbsp snipped fresh chives

pepper

12 sheets filo pastry

100 g/3¹/2 oz butter, melted, plus extra for greasing

4 tbsp dried breadcrumbs

6 tsp fennel seeds

method

1 In a large bowl, combine the feta, ricotta, smoked salmon, dill and chives. Season with pepper.

2 Lay out a sheet of pastry on the work surface and brush well with melted butter. Sprinkle over 2 teaspoons of the breadcrumbs and cover with a second sheet of pastry. Brush with butter and spread a large tablespoon of the salmon mixture on one end of the pastry. Roll the pastry up, folding in the sides, to enclose the salmon completely and create a neat parcel. Place on a lightly greased baking sheet, brush the top of the parcel with butter and sprinkle over 1 teaspoon of the fennel seeds. Repeat with the remaining ingredients to make 6 parcels.

3 Bake the parcels in a preheated oven, 180°C/350°F/Gas Mark 4, for 25–30 minutes, or until the pastry is golden brown. Serve warm.

crab & watercress tart

ingredients

SERVES 6

pastry

4 tbsp cold butter, diced,
plus extra for greasing

125 g/4^{1}/$_2$ oz plain flour, plus
extra for dusting

pinch of salt

ice-cold water

filling

300 g/10^{1}/$_2$ oz fresh white
and brown crabmeat,
thawed if frozen

1 bunch of watercress, leaves
picked from the stems

50 ml/2 fl oz milk

2 large eggs plus 3 egg yolks

200 ml/7 fl oz double cream

salt and pepper

^{1}/$_2$ tsp ground nutmeg

^{1}/$_2$ bunch of fresh chives,
snipped

2 tbsp freshly grated
Parmesan cheese

method

1 Lightly grease a 23-cm/9-inch loose-based fluted tart tin. Sift the flour with the salt into a food processor, add the butter and process until the mixture resembles fine breadcrumbs. Tip the mixture into a large bowl and add a little cold water, just enough to bring the dough together. Turn out onto a lightly floured work surface. Roll out to 8 cm/3^{1}/4 inches larger than the tin. Line the tin with the dough and trim the edge. Line the tart shell with baking paper and fill with dried beans. Chill in the refrigerator for 30 minutes.

2 Remove the tart shell from the refrigerator and bake in a preheated oven, 190°C/375°F/ Gas Mark 5, for 10 minutes. Remove the paper and beans and bake the tart shell for 5 minutes more. Remove from the oven and reduce the oven temperature to 325°F/160°C/Gas Mark 3.

3 Arrange the crabmeat and watercress in the tart shell, reserving a few watercress leaves for garnishing. Whisk the milk, eggs and egg yolks together in a bowl. Bring the cream to simmering point in a saucepan and pour over the egg mixture, whisking all the time. Season with salt and pepper and stir in the nutmeg and chives. Carefully pour over the crab and watercress and sprinkle over the cheese. Bake for 35–40 minutes until golden and set. Let the tart rest for 10 minutes before serving, garnished with the reserved watercress.

main meals

One of the most rewarding aspects of making fish the centrepiece of your main meal is that it requires so little in the way of cooking, yet looks as if you've put in a huge amount of effort! Add a simple sauce and you have a taste sensation. Monkfish with Lime & Chilli Sauce is a delectable example that takes little more than five minutes to prepare and cook – in fact, cooking the rice to accompany it will take longer!

Roasting is a delicious and trouble-free way to cook fish. Try Roast Monkfish with Romesco Sauce, Italian Fish, Garlic-crusted Roast Haddock, Roast Red Snapper with Fennel, Roast Salmon with Lemon & Herbs, or Roast Tuna with Orange & Anchovies. It is also wonderful in stews such as Spanish Swordfish Stew or Moroccan Fish Tagine, which is served with couscous.

Fish goes beautifully with butter, although this somewhat cancels out the virtue of its being low in fat! For the occasional treat, however, serve Sole à la Meunière or Skate in Black Butter Sauce, and schedule in a brisk walk to follow!

For something a little different, try Fish with Yucatan Flavours – swordfish steaks marinated in a spicy, herby, fruity dressing, then steamed in banana leaves. Very tasty, and a great talking point when you serve each portion of fish in its leaf!

monkfish with lime & chilli sauce

ingredients

SERVES 4

4 x 115-g/4-oz
   monkfish fillets
25 g/1 oz rice flour
   or cornflour
6 tbsp vegetable or peanut oil
4 garlic cloves, crushed
2 large fresh red chillies,
   deseeded and sliced
2 tsp soft light brown sugar
juice of 2 limes
grated rind of 1 lime
freshly boiled rice, to serve

method

1 Toss the fish in the flour, shaking off any excess. Heat the oil in a wok or frying pan and cook the fish on all sides until browned and cooked through, taking care when turning not to break it up.

2 Lift the fish out of the wok and keep warm. Add the garlic and chillies and stir-fry for 1–2 minutes, until they have softened.

3 Add the sugar, the lime juice and rind, and 2–3 tablespoons of water and bring to the boil. Simmer gently for 1–2 minutes, then spoon the mixture over the fish. Serve immediately with freshly boiled rice.

roast monkfish with romesco sauce

ingredients

SERVES 4

1 monkfish tail, about
    900 g/2 lb, membrane
    removed
2–3 slices serrano ham
olive oil, for brushing
salt and pepper

romesco sauce

1 red pepper, halved
    and deseeded
4 garlic cloves, unpeeled
2 tomatoes, halved
125 ml/4 fl oz olive oil
1 slice white bread, diced
4 tbsp blanched almonds
1 fresh red chilli, deseeded
    and chopped
2 shallots, chopped
1 tsp paprika
2 tbsp red wine vinegar
2 tsp sugar
1 tbsp water

method

1 Place the pepper, garlic and tomatoes in a roasting tin and toss with 1 tablespoon of the oil. Roast in a preheated oven, 220°C/425°F/ Gas Mark 7, for 20–25 minutes, then cover with a tea towel, and set aside for 10 minutes. Peel off the skins and place the vegetables in a food processor.

2 Heat 1 tablespoon of the remaining oil in a frying pan. Cook the bread and almonds over a low heat, stirring constantly, until golden. Remove with a slotted spoon and drain on kitchen paper. Add the chilli, shallots and paprika to the frying pan and cook, stirring, for 5 minutes. Transfer both mixtures to the food processor, add the vinegar, sugar and water, and process to a paste. With the motor running, add the remaining oil through the feeder tube.

3 Reduce the oven temperature to 200°C/ 400°F/Gas Mark 6. Rinse the monkfish tail and pat it dry. Wrap the ham around the monkfish, brush lightly with oil and season. Place the fish on a baking sheet and roast for 20 minutes until the flesh is opaque and flakes easily.

4 Cut through the ham to remove the central bone and produce 2 thick fillets. Cut each fillet into 2 pieces and arrange on plates with a spoonful of the sauce. Serve immediately.

spanish swordfish stew

ingredients

SERVES 4

4 tbsp olive oil

3 shallots, chopped

2 garlic cloves, chopped

225 g/8 oz canned chopped
    tomatoes

1 tbsp tomato paste

650 g/1 lb 7 oz potatoes,
    sliced

250 ml/9 fl oz vegetable stock

2 tbsp lemon juice

1 red pepper, deseeded and
    chopped

1 orange pepper, deseeded
    and chopped

20 black olives, pitted
    and halved

1 kg/2 lb 4 oz swordfish
    steak, skinned and cut
    into bite-sized pieces

salt and pepper

parsley springs and lemon
    slices, to garnish

method

1 Heat the oil in a saucepan over a low heat, add the shallots and cook, stirring frequently, for 4 minutes, or until softened. Add the garlic, tomatoes and tomato paste, cover and simmer gently for 20 minutes.

2 Meanwhile, put the potatoes in an ovenproof casserole with the stock and lemon juice. Bring to the boil, then reduce the heat and add the peppers. Cover and cook for 15 minutes.

3 Add the olives, swordfish and the tomato mixture to the potatoes. Season with salt and pepper. Stir well, then cover and simmer for 7–10 minutes, or until the swordfish is cooked to your taste.

4 Remove from the heat and garnish with parsley sprigs and lemon slices.

fish with yucatan flavours

ingredients

SERVES 8

4 tbsp annatto seeds, soaked
    in water overnight

3 garlic cloves, finely chopped

1 tbsp mild chilli powder

1 tbsp paprika

1 tsp ground cumin

1/2 tsp dried oregano

2 tbsp beer or tequila

juice of 1 lime and 1 orange
    or 3 tbsp pineapple juice

2 tbsp olive oil

2 tbsp chopped fresh
    coriander

1/4 tsp ground cinnamon

1/4 tsp ground cloves

1 kg/2 lb 4 oz swordfish
    steaks

banana leaves, for wrapping
    (optional)

orange wedges, to serve

method

1 Drain the annatto, then crush them to a paste in a mortar with a pestle. Work in the garlic, chilli powder, paprika, cumin, oregano, beer or tequila, fruit juice, olive oil, coriander, cinnamon and cloves. Smear the paste onto the fish and marinate in the refrigerator for at least 3 hours or overnight.

2 Wrap the fish steaks in banana leaves, if using, tying with string to make parcels. Bring water to the boil in a steamer, then add a batch of parcels to the top part of the steamer and cook for about 15 minutes or until the fish is cooked through.

3 Alternatively, cook the fish without wrapping in the banana leaves. To cook on the barbecue, place in a hinged basket, or on a rack, and cook over the hot coals for 5–6 minutes on each side until cooked through; or cook the fish under a preheated grill for 5–6 minutes on each side until cooked through.

4 Serve with orange wedges for squeezing over the fish.

italian fish

ingredients

SERVES 4

2 tbsp butter

50 g/1³/₄ oz fresh wholemeal
    breadcrumbs

1 heaped tbsp
    chopped walnuts

grated rind and juice of
    2 lemons

2 fresh rosemary sprigs,
    stalks removed

2 tbsp chopped fresh parsley

4 cod fillets, about
    150 g/5¹/₂ oz each

1 garlic clove, crushed

1 small fresh red chilli, diced

3 tbsp walnut oil

method

1 Melt the butter in a large saucepan over
a low heat, stirring constantly. Remove the
pan from the heat and add the breadcrumbs,
walnuts, the rind and juice of 1 lemon, half
the rosemary and half the parsley, stirring
until mixed.

2 Press the breadcrumb mixture over the
top of the cod fillets. Place the cod fillets in
a shallow foil-lined roasting tin and roast in a
preheated oven, 200°C/400°F/Gas Mark 6,
for 25–30 minutes.

3 Mix the garlic, the remaining lemon rind
and juice, rosemary and parsley, and the chilli
together in a bowl. Beat in the oil and mix to
combine. Drizzle the dressing over the cod
steaks as soon as they are cooked.

4 Transfer the fish to warmed serving plates
and serve immediately.

baked lemon cod with herb sauce

ingredients

SERVES 4

4 thick cod fillets

olive oil, for brushing

8 thin lemon slices

salt and pepper

herb sauce

4 tbsp olive oil

1 garlic clove, crushed

4 tbsp chopped fresh parsley

2 tbsp chopped fresh mint

juice of $1/2$ lemon

method

1 Rinse each cod fillet and pat dry with kitchen paper, then brush with oil. Place each fillet on a piece of baking paper large enough to encase the fish in a parcel. Top each fillet with 2 lemon slices and season with salt and pepper. Fold over the baking paper to encase the fish and bake in a preheated oven, 200°C/400°F/Gas Mark 6, for 20 minutes, or until just cooked and opaque.

2 Meanwhile, to make the herb sauce, put all the ingredients into a food processor and process until finely chopped. Season with salt and pepper.

3 Carefully unfold each parcel and place it on a serving plate. Pour a spoonful of herb sauce over each piece of fish before serving.

cod with catalan spinach

ingredients

SERVES 4

55 g/2 oz raisins

55 g/2 oz pine kernels

4 tbsp extra virgin olive oil

3 garlic cloves, crushed

500 g/1 lb 2 oz baby spinach
    leaves, rinsed and
    shaken dry

4 cod fillets, each about
    175 g/6 oz

olive oil

salt and pepper

tomato halves and lemon
    wedges, to serve

method

1 Put the raisins in a small bowl, cover with hot water and set aside to soak for 15 minutes; drain well.

2 Meanwhile, put the pine kernels in a dry frying pan over a medium–high heat and dry-fry for 1–2 minutes, shaking frequently, until toasted and golden brown: watch closely because they burn quickly.

3 Heat the oil in a large, lidded frying pan over a medium–high heat. Add the garlic and cook for 2 minutes, or until golden but not brown. Remove with a slotted spoon and discard.

4 Add the spinach to the oil with only the rinsing water clinging to its leaves. Cover and cook for 4–5 minutes until wilted. Uncover, stir in the drained raisins and pine kernels and continue cooking until all the liquid evaporates. Season with salt and pepper and keep warm.

5 To cook the cod, brush the fillets lightly with oil and sprinkle with salt and pepper. Place under a preheated hot grill about 10 cm/ 4 inches from the heat and grill for 8–10 minutes until the flesh is opaque and flakes easily.

6 Divide the spinach between 4 plates and place the cod fillets on top. Serve with the tomato halves and lemon wedges.

garlic-crusted roast haddock

ingredients

SERVES 4

900 g/2 lb floury potatoes

125 ml/4 fl oz milk

55 g/2 oz butter

salt and pepper

4 haddock fillets, about
    225 g/8 oz each

1 tbsp corn oil

4 garlic cloves, finely chopped

2 tbsp chopped fresh parsley,
    to garnish

method

1 Cut the potatoes into chunks and cook in a saucepan of lightly salted water for 15 minutes, or until tender. Drain well. Mash in the pan until smooth. Set over a low heat and beat in the milk, butter, and salt and pepper.

2 Place the haddock fillets in a roasting tin and brush the fish with the oil. Sprinkle the garlic on top, add salt and pepper to taste, then spread with the mashed potatoes. Roast in a preheated oven, 230°C/450°F/Gas Mark 8, for 8–10 minutes, or until the fish is just tender.

3 Meanwhile, preheat the grill. Transfer the fish to the grill and cook for about 2 minutes, or until golden brown. Sprinkle with the chopped parsley and serve immediately.

sole à la meunière

ingredients

SERVES 4

4 tbsp plain flour

1 tsp salt

4 x 400-g/14-oz Dover sole,
    cleaned and skinned

150 g/5^1/$_2$ oz butter

3 tbsp lemon juice

1 tbsp chopped fresh parsley

^{1}/$_4$ of a preserved lemon,
    finely chopped (optional)

fresh parsley sprigs, to garnish

lemon wedges, to serve

method

1 Mix the flour with the salt and place on a large plate. Drop the fish into the flour, one at a time, and shake well to remove any excess. Melt 3 tablespoons of the butter in a small saucepan and use to brush the fish liberally all over. Place the fish under a grill preheated to medium and cook for 5 minutes on each side.

2 Meanwhile, melt the remaining butter in a saucepan. Pour cold water into a bowl that is large enough to take the bottom of the saucepan and keep near by.

3 Heat the butter until it turns a golden brown and begins to smell nutty. Remove from the heat immediately and immerse the bottom of the saucepan in the cold water, to stop the cooking.

4 Place the fillets on individual plates, drizzle with the lemon juice and sprinkle with the parsley and preserved lemon, if using. Pour over the browned butter, garnish with parsley sprigs and serve immediately with lemon wedges for squeezing over.

skate in black butter sauce

ingredients

SERVES 4

4 skate wings, about
    175 g/6 oz each
600 ml/1 pint fish stock
225 ml/8 fl oz dry white wine
salt and pepper
4 tbsp butter
2 tbsp lemon juice
2 tsp capers in brine, rinsed
2 tbsp chopped fresh parsley

method

1 Put the fish in a large, heavy-based frying pan or ovenproof casserole, pour in the stock and wine, and season with salt and pepper. Bring to the boil, then reduce the heat and simmer for 10–15 minutes until the fish is tender.

2 Meanwhile, melt the butter in a large, heavy-based frying pan over a very low heat and cook until it turns brown but not black. Stir in the lemon juice, capers and parsley and heat for a further 1–2 minutes.

3 Transfer the skate wings to warmed serving plates with a spatula, pour the black butter sauce over and serve immediately.

moroccan fish tagine

ingredients

SERVES 4

2 tbsp olive oil

1 large onion, finely chopped

large pinch of saffron threads

1/2 tsp ground cinnamon

1 tsp ground coriander

1/2 tsp ground cumin

1/2 tsp ground turmeric

200 g/7 oz canned chopped
    tomatoes

300 ml/10 fl oz fish stock

4 small red snapper, cleaned,
    boned, and heads and
    tails removed

50 g/1 3/4 oz pitted green
    olives

1 tbsp chopped preserved
    lemon

3 tbsp chopped fresh
    coriander

salt and pepper

freshly prepared couscous,
    to serve

method

1 Heat the oil in a large saucepan or ovenproof casserole over a low heat, add the onion and cook, stirring occasionally, for 10 minutes until softened but not browned. Add the saffron, cinnamon, coriander, cumin and turmeric and cook, stirring constantly, for a further 30 seconds.

2 Add the tomatoes and stock and stir well. Bring to the boil, then reduce the heat, cover and simmer for 15 minutes. Uncover and simmer for a further 20–35 minutes, until thickened.

3 Cut each snapper in half, then add the pieces to the pan, pushing them into the sauce. Simmer gently for a further 5–6 minutes until the fish is just cooked.

4 Carefully stir in the olives, preserved lemon and coriander. Season with salt and pepper and serve with couscous.

blackened snapper with sweetcorn papaya relish

ingredients

SERVES 4

4 x 85-g/3-oz snapper fillets

vegetable oil spray

2 lemons, halved, to serve

relish

2 tbsp finely chopped onion

1 tsp sugar

2 tbsp white wine vinegar

2 tbsp cooked or canned
    sweetcorn kernels

$1/4$ tsp finely chopped
    habanero chilli or other
    type of chilli

100 ml/$3^1/2$ fl oz water

$1/4$ tsp yellow mustard seeds

pinch of ground turmeric

1 tsp cornflour, blended with
    a little cold water

50 g/$1^3/4$ oz papaya, cut into
    5-mm/$1/4$-inch cubes

seasoning mix

$1/4$ tsp paprika

$1/2$ tsp onion powder

$1/4$ tsp dried thyme

$1/4$ tsp dried oregano

$1/4$ tsp cayenne pepper

$1/4$ tsp pepper

$1/2$ tsp cornflour

method

1 To make the relish, place the onion, sugar, vinegar, sweetcorn, chilli, water, mustard seeds and turmeric in a small saucepan over a medium heat and bring to the boil. Simmer for 10 minutes, then add the cornflour mixture, stirring constantly, and cook until it is the required consistency (it will thicken slightly when cooled). Stir in the papaya and cool.

2 To make the seasoning mix, put all the ingredients into a bowl and mix thoroughly.

3 Sprinkle the seasoning mix over the snapper fillets on both sides and pat into the flesh, then shake off any excess. Lay the fillets on a board.

4 Heat a non-stick frying pan over a high heat until smoking. Lightly spray both sides of the fillets with oil, then put into the hot frying pan and cook for 2 minutes. Turn the fillets and cook all the way through. (If the fillets are thick, finish the cooking under a preheated grill as the less intense heat will prevent the seasoning mix from burning.) Remove the fish from the frying pan.

5 Add the lemon halves, cut-side down, and cook over a high heat for 2–5 minutes, until browned. Serve the fillets, topped with relish, on warmed plates, with the lemon halves.

roast red snapper with fennel

ingredients

SERVES 4

250 g/9 oz dried, white
    breadcrumbs

2 tbsp milk

1 fennel bulb, thinly sliced,
    fronds reserved for garnish

1 tbsp lemon juice

2 tbsp sambuca

1 tbsp chopped fresh thyme

1 bay leaf, crumbled

1.5 kg/3 lb 5 oz whole red
    snapper, cleaned, scaled
    and boned

salt and pepper

3 tbsp olive oil, plus extra for
    brushing

1 red onion, chopped

300 ml/10 fl oz dry white wine

method

1 Place the breadcrumbs in a bowl, add the milk and set aside for 5 minutes to soak. Place the fennel in another bowl and add the lemon juice, sambuca, thyme and bay leaf. Squeeze the breadcrumbs and add them to the mixture, stirring well.

2 Rinse the fish inside and out under cold running water and pat dry with kitchen paper. Season with salt and pepper. Spoon the fennel mixture into the cavity, then bind the fish with trussing thread or kitchen string.

3 Brush a large ovenproof dish with olive oil and sprinkle the onion over the bottom. Lay the fish on top and pour in the wine – it should reach about one third of the way up the fish. Drizzle the red snapper with the olive oil and cook in preheated oven, 190ºC/375°F/ Gas Mark 5, for 25–30 minutes. Baste the fish occasionally with the cooking juices and if it starts to brown, cover with a piece of foil to protect it.

4 Carefully lift out the fish, remove the string and place on a warmed serving platter. Garnish with the reserved fennel fronds and serve immediately.

grilled sea bass
with stewed artichokes

ingredients

SERVES 4

1.8 kg/4 lb baby globe
    artichokes
2¹/₂ tbsp fresh lemon juice,
    plus the cut halves of
    the lemon
150 ml/5 fl oz olive oil, plus
    1 tbsp, for brushing
10 garlic cloves, finely sliced
1 tbsp chopped fresh thyme,
    plus extra to garnish
salt and pepper
6 x 115-g/4-oz sea bass fillets
crusty bread, to serve

method

1 Peel away the tough outer leaves of each
artichoke until the yellow-green heart is
revealed. Slice off the pointed top at about
halfway between the point and the top of the
stem. Cut off the stem and pare off what is
left of the dark green leaves around the
bottom of the artichoke.

2 Submerge the prepared artichokes in
water containing the cut halves of the lemon
to prevent discolouration. When all the
artichokes have been prepared, turn them
choke side down and slice thickly.

3 Heat the olive oil in a large saucepan. Add
the artichoke pieces, garlic, thyme, lemon
juice, salt and pepper, cover and cook the
artichokes over a low heat for 20–30 minutes,
without colouring, until tender.

4 Meanwhile, preheat a ridged griddle pan or
light a barbecue. Brush the sea bass fillets
with the 1 tablespoon of olive oil and season
well. Cook on the griddle pan or over hot coals
for 3–4 minutes on each side until just tender.

5 Divide the stewed artichokes between
individual plates and top each with a fish fillet.
Garnish with chopped thyme and serve with
crusty bread.

sweet-&-sour sea bass

ingredients

SERVES 2

60 g/2¹/4 oz pak choi,
  shredded
40 g/1¹/2 oz beansprouts
40 g/1¹/2 oz shiitake
  mushrooms, sliced
40 g/1¹/2 oz oyster
  mushrooms, torn
20 g/³/4 oz spring onions,
  finely sliced
1 tsp finely grated fresh
  ginger
1 tbsp finely sliced
  lemon grass
2 x 90-g/3¹/4-oz sea bass
  fillets, skinned and boned
10 g/¹/4 oz sesame seeds,
  toasted

sweet-&-sour sauce

90 ml/3 fl oz unsweetened
  pineapple juice
1 tbsp sugar
1 tbsp red wine vinegar
2 star anise, crushed
6 tbsp tomato juice
1 tbsp cornflour, blended with
  a little cold water

method

1 Cut 2 x 38-cm/15-inch squares of baking paper and 2 x 38-cm/15-inch squares of aluminium foil.

2 To make the sauce, heat the pineapple juice, sugar, red wine vinegar, star anise and tomato juice. Simmer for 1–2 minutes, then thicken with the cornflour and water mixture, whisking continuously. Pass through a fine sieve into a small bowl to cool.

3 In a separate large bowl mix together the pak choi, beansprouts, mushrooms and spring onions, then add the ginger and lemon grass. Toss all the ingredients together.

4 Put a square of greaseproof paper on top of a square of foil and fold into a triangle. Open up and place half the vegetable mix in the centre, pour half the sweet and sour sauce over the vegetables and place the sea bass on top. Sprinkle with a few sesame seeds. Close the triangle over the mixture and, starting at the top, fold the right corner and crumple the edges together to form an airtight triangular bag. Repeat to make another bag.

5 Place on a baking sheet and cook in a preheated oven, 200°C/400°F/Gas Mark 6, for 10 minutes, until the foil bags puff with steam. To serve, place on individual plates and snip open at the table.

seared salmon with quick hollandaise sauce

ingredients

SERVES 4

1 tbsp dried thyme

1 tbsp dried rosemary

1 tbsp dried oregano

1 tbsp mild paprika

1 tsp garlic powder

2 tsp cumin seeds

1 tbsp sea salt

4 salmon fillets, skin removed

1 tbsp vegetable oil

150 g/5^{1}/$_{2}$ oz baby spinach

quick hollandaise sauce

3 egg yolks

200 g/7 oz butter

1 tbsp lemon juice

pepper

method

1 Combine the dried herbs, paprika, garlic powder, cumin seeds and sea salt in a small grinder and process until smooth. Alternatively, grind by hand using a pestle in a mortar. Rub 1 tablespoon of the mixture into the top of each of the salmon fillets.

2 Heat the oil in a large frying pan and cook the salmon, spice-side down, for 2–3 minutes, or until golden brown. Turn over and continue cooking until the salmon is cooked to your liking. Do not overcook or the salmon will be dry.

3 To make the hollandaise sauce, place the egg yolks in a blender or food processor. Melt the butter in a small saucepan until bubbling. With the motor running, gradually add the hot butter in a steady stream until the sauce is thick and creamy. Add the lemon juice, and a little warm water if the sauce is too thick, then season with pepper. Remove from the blender or food processor and keep warm.

4 Divide the baby spinach equally between 4 plates, place the cooked salmon on top, and spoon over the sauce. Serve immediately.

roast salmon with lemon & herbs

ingredients

SERVES 4

6 tbsp extra virgin olive oil

1 onion, sliced

1 leek, sliced

juice of $1/2$ lemon

2 tbsp chopped fresh parsley

2 tbsp chopped fresh dill

salt and pepper

500 g/1 lb 2 oz salmon fillets

freshly cooked baby spinach
    leaves, to serve

lemon slices, to garnish

method

1 Heat 1 tablespoon of the oil in a frying pan over a medium heat. Add the onion and leek and cook, stirring occasionally, for 4 minutes, or until slightly softened.

2 Meanwhile, place the remaining oil in a small bowl with the lemon juice and herbs and season with salt and pepper. Stir together well. Rinse the fish under cold running water, then pat dry with kitchen paper. Arrange the fish in a shallow ovenproof dish.

3 Remove the frying pan from the heat and spread the onion and leek over the fish. Pour the oil mixture over the top, making sure that everything is well coated. Roast in the centre of a preheated oven, 200°C/400°F/Gas Mark 6, for 10 minutes, or until the fish is cooked through.

4 Arrange the cooked spinach on serving plates. Remove the fish and vegetables and serve next to the spinach, with the vegetables arranged on top of the fish. Garnish with lemon slices and serve immediately.

ginger-marinated salmon & scallops

ingredients

SERVES 4

200 g/7 oz brown basmati
  rice

1/2 cucumber, diced

4 spring onions, sliced

1/2 bunch fresh coriander,
  chopped

1 red pepper, deseeded
  and diced

1 fresh green chilli, deseeded
  and thinly sliced

juice of 1 lime

2 tbsp toasted sesame oil

500 g/1 lb 2 oz salmon
  fillet, skinned and cut into
  chunks

8 scallops, without corals,
  cleaned

50 g/1³/₄ oz fresh ginger

juice of 1 lemon

1 tbsp olive oil

green salad, to serve

method

1 Bring a large saucepan of water to the boil, add the rice and cook for 25 minutes, or until tender. Drain and cool. Mix the cooled rice with the cucumber, spring onions, coriander, red pepper, chilli, lime juice and sesame oil in a bowl. Cover and set aside to allow the flavours to develop.

2 Meanwhile, put the salmon chunks into a shallow, non-metallic bowl. Cut each scallop in half and add to the bowl. Using a garlic press or the back of a knife, crush the ginger to extract the juice. Mix the ginger juice with the lemon juice and olive oil in a small bowl or jug and pour over the seafood. Turn the seafood to coat in the marinade. Cover and marinate in the refrigerator for 30 minutes. Soak 8 wooden skewers in cold water for 30 minutes, then drain.

3 Thread an equal quantity of the salmon and scallops onto the skewers. Cook under a grill preheated to high for 3–4 minutes on each side, or until cooked through. Serve the hot seafood skewers with the rice salad and a green salad.

mexican-style salmon

ingredients

SERVES 4

4 salmon steaks, about
175–225 g/6–8 oz each
lime slices, to garnish

marinade

4 garlic cloves, finely chopped
2 tbsp extra virgin olive oil
pinch of ground allspice
pinch of ground cinnamon
juice of 2 limes
1–2 tsp marinade from
    canned chipotle chillies or
    bottled chipotle chilli salsa
1/4 tsp ground cumin
pinch of sugar
salt and pepper

to serve

tomato wedges
3 finely chopped spring
    onions
shredded lettuce

method

1 To make the marinade, place the garlic in a bowl with the olive oil, allspice, cinnamon, lime juice, chipotle marinade, cumin and sugar. Add salt and pepper and stir to combine.

2 Coat the salmon with the garlic mixture, then place in a non-metallic dish. Leave to marinate for at least 1 hour or overnight in the refrigerator.

3 Transfer to a grill pan and cook under a preheated grill for 3–4 minutes on each side. Alternatively, cook the salmon over hot coals on a barbecue until cooked through.

4 To serve, mix the tomato wedges with the spring onions. Place the salmon on individual plates and arrange the tomato salad and shredded lettuce alongside. Garnish with lime slices and serve.

roast tuna
with orange & anchovies

ingredients

SERVES 4–6

200 ml/7 fl oz freshly
squeezed orange juice

3 tbsp extra virgin olive oil

55 g/2 oz anchovy fillets in oil,
roughly chopped, with the
oil reserved

small pinch of dried red
pepper flakes, or to taste

pepper

1 tuna fillet, about
600 g/1 lb 5 oz

method

1 In a large, non-metallic bowl, combine the orange juice, 2 tablespoons of the olive oil, the anchovies and their oil, and the red pepper flakes and season with pepper. Add the tuna and spoon the marinade over it. Cover with clingfilm and marinate in the refrigerator for 2 hours, turning the tuna occasionally. Remove from the refrigerator about 20 minutes before cooking to return the fish to room temperature.

2 Remove the tuna from the marinade, reserving the marinade, and wipe dry. Heat the remaining oil in a large frying pan over a high heat. Add the tuna and sear for 1 minute on each side until lightly browned and crisp. Place in a roasting tin. Cover the tin tightly with foil.

3 Roast in a preheated oven, 220°C/425°F/ Gas Mark 7, for 8 minutes for medium–rare and 10 minutes for medium–well done. Remove from the oven and set aside to rest for 2 minutes before slicing.

4 Meanwhile, place the marinade in a small saucepan over a high heat and bring to a rolling boil. Boil for 2 minutes.

5 Transfer the tuna to a serving platter and carve into thick slices, which will probably break into chunks as you cut them. Serve the sauce separately for spooning over.

chargrilled tuna with chilli salsa

ingredients

SERVES 4

4 tuna steaks, about
    175 g/6 oz each

grated rind and juice of 1 lime

2 tbsp olive oil

salt and pepper

green salad, to serve

chilli salsa

2 orange peppers

1 tbsp olive oil

juice of 1 lime

juice of 1 orange

2–3 fresh red chillies,
    deseeded and chopped

pinch of cayenne pepper

method

1 Rinse the tuna thoroughly under cold running water and pat dry with kitchen paper, then place in a large shallow non-metallic dish. Sprinkle the lime rind and juice and the oil over the fish. Season with salt and pepper, cover with clingfilm and marinate in the refrigerator for up to 1 hour.

2 Preheat the barbecue. To make the salsa, brush the peppers with the olive oil and cook over hot coals, turning frequently, for 10 minutes, or until the skin is blackened and charred. Remove from the grill and cool slightly, then peel off the skins and discard the seeds. Place the peppers in a food processor with the remaining salsa ingredients and process to a purée. Transfer to a bowl and season with salt and pepper.

3 Cook the tuna over hot coals for 4–5 minutes on each side until golden. Transfer to plates, and serve immediately with the green salad and the salsa.

rice, pasta & noodles

Italy and Spain are bordered by miles of Mediterranean coastline, so it is not surprising that fish features prominently in the culinary tradition of these two countries. Fish and seafood go into what has almost become Spain's national dish – paella. It often includes meat, usually chicken, too, but Paella with Mussels & White Wine and Seafood Paella with Lemon & Herbs make the most of the daily catch from the sea. The classic Italian rice dish, risotto – a gloriously creamy, rich delight – also works wonderfully well with fish and seafood. Prawn & Asparagus Risotto and Saffron & Lemon Risotto with Scallops are both simple yet sophisticated, and if you love things in shells, Venetian Seafood Risotto is packed with prawns, mussels and clams.

Pasta, another Italian favourite, is also a great partner for fish. Smoked salmon goes especially well – try Fettucine with Smoked Salmon or Linguine with Smoked Salmon & Rocket, both light, delicious recipes. Noodles, the Asian version of pasta, are particularly useful if you have a gluten intolerance – you can choose recipes such as Fish Curry with Rice Noodles, Thai Fisherman's Catch, Malaysian-style Coconut Noodles with Prawns and Prawn Laksa, which have all the satisfying texture of noodles but not a hint of wheat!

paella with mussels & white wine

ingredients

SERVES 4–6

150 g/5^1/$_2$ oz cod fillet,
skinned and rinsed in cold
water

1.3 litres/2^1/$_4$ pints simmering
fish stock

200 g/7 oz live mussels,
prepared (see page 32)

3 tbsp olive oil

1 large red onion, chopped

2 garlic cloves, crushed

^{1}/$_2$ tsp cayenne pepper

^{1}/$_2$ tsp saffron threads infused
in 2 tbsp hot water

225 g/8 oz tomatoes, peeled
and cut into wedges

1 red pepper, deseeded
and sliced

1 green pepper, deseeded
and sliced

375 g/13 oz medium-grain
paella rice

100 ml/3^1/$_2$ fl oz white wine

150 g/5^1/$_2$ oz shelled peas

1 tbsp chopped fresh dill,
plus extra to garnish

salt and pepper

lemon wedges, to serve

method

1 Cook the cod in the saucepan of simmering stock for 5 minutes. Transfer the cod to a colander, rinse under cold running water and drain. Cut into chunks, then transfer to a bowl. Cook the mussels in the stock for 5 minutes, or until opened, then transfer to the bowl with the cod, discarding any that remain closed.

2 Heat the oil in a paella pan and stir in the onion over a medium heat until softened. Add the garlic, cayenne pepper and saffron and its soaking liquid and cook, stirring constantly, for 1 minute. Add the tomatoes and peppers and cook, stirring, for 2 minutes.

3 Add the rice and cook, stirring, for 1 minute. Add the wine and most of the stock and bring to the boil, then simmer for 10 minutes. Do not stir during cooking, but shake the pan once or twice and when adding ingredients. Add the peas, dill, salt and pepper. Cook for 10 minutes, or until the rice is almost cooked, adding more stock if necessary. Add the cod and mussels and cook for 3 minutes.

4 When all the liquid has been absorbed and you detect a faint toasty aroma coming from the rice, remove from the heat immediately. Cover with foil and stand for 5 minutes. Garnish with dill and serve with lemon wedges.

seafood paella with lemon & herbs

ingredients

SERVES 4–6

1/2 tsp saffron threads

2 tbsp hot water

150 g/5 1/2 oz cod fillet, skinned and rinsed under cold running water

1.2 litres/2 pints simmering fish stock

12 large raw prawns, peeled and deveined

450 g/1 lb raw squid, cleaned and cut into rings or bite-sized pieces (or use the same quantity of shucked scallops)

3 tbsp olive oil

1 large red onion, chopped

2 garlic cloves, crushed

1 small fresh red chilli, deseeded and minced

225 g/8 oz tomatoes, peeled and cut into wedges

375 g/13 oz medium-grain paella rice

1 tbsp chopped fresh parsley

2 tsp chopped fresh dill

salt and pepper

1 lemon, cut into halves, to serve

method

1 Put the saffron threads and water in a small bowl to infuse for a few minutes.

2 Add the cod to the saucepan of simmering stock and cook for 5 minutes, then transfer to a colander, rinse under cold running water and drain. Add the prawns and squid to the stock and cook for 2 minutes. Cut the cod into chunks, then transfer with the other seafood to a bowl and set aside. Let the stock simmer.

3 Heat the oil in a paella pan and stir in the onion over a medium heat until softened. Add the garlic, chilli and saffron and its soaking liquid and cook, stirring, for 1 minute. Add the tomato wedges and cook, stirring, for 2 minutes. Add the rice and herbs and cook, stirring, for 1 minute. Add most of the stock and bring to the boil. Simmer, uncovered, for 10 minutes. Do not stir during cooking, but shake the pan once or twice and when adding ingredients. Season and cook for 10 minutes, until the rice is almost cooked. Add more stock if necessary. Add the seafood and cook for 2 minutes.

4 When all the liquid has been absorbed and you detect a faint toasty aroma coming from the rice, remove from the heat immediately. Cover with foil and stand for 5 minutes. Serve with the lemon halves.

venetian seafood risotto

ingredients

SERVES 4

225 g/8 oz prepared raw
    prawns, heads and
    shells reserved
2 garlic cloves, halved
1 lemon, sliced
225 g/8 oz live mussels,
    scrubbed and debearded
225 g/8 oz live clams,
    scrubbed
600 ml/1 pint water
115 g/4 oz butter
1 tbsp olive oil
1 onion, finely chopped
2 tbsp chopped fresh
    flat-leaf parsley
350 g/12 oz arborio rice
125 ml/4 fl oz dry white wine
225 g/8 oz cleaned raw squid,
    cut into small pieces, or
    squid rings
4 tbsp Marsala
salt and pepper

method

1 Wrap the prawn heads and shells in a square of muslin and pound with a pestle. Put the wrapped shells and their liquid in a saucepan with the garlic, lemon, mussels and clams. Add the water, cover and bring to the boil over a high heat. Cook, shaking the pan frequently, for 5 minutes until the shellfish have opened. Discard any that remain closed. Cool, then shell and set aside. Strain the cooking liquid through a muslin-lined sieve and add water to make 1.2 litres/2 pints. Bring to the boil in a saucepan, then simmer over a low heat.

2 Melt 2 tablespoons of butter with the olive oil in a saucepan. Cook the onion and half the parsley over a medium heat, stirring, until softened. Reduce the heat, stir in the rice and cook, stirring, until the grains are translucent. Add the wine and cook, stirring, for 1 minute. Add the hot cooking liquid a ladleful at a time, stirring constantly, until all the liquid is absorbed and the rice is creamy.

3 Melt 55 g/2 oz of the remaining butter in a pan. Cook the squid, stirring frequently, for 3 minutes. Add the prawns and cook for 2–3 minutes, until the squid is opaque and the prawns have changed colour. Add the Marsala, bring to the boil, and cook until the liquid has evaporated. Stir all the seafood into the rice, add the remaining butter and parsley, and season. Heat gently and serve immediately.

lobster risotto

ingredients

SERVES 2

1 cooked lobster, about
    400–450 g/14 oz–1 lb
1 tbsp olive oil
55 g/2 oz butter
1/2 onion, finely chopped
1 garlic clove, finely chopped
1 tsp chopped fresh thyme
    leaves
175 g/6 oz arborio rice
150 ml/5 fl oz sparkling white
    wine
600 ml/1 pint simmering
    fish stock
1 tsp green or pink
    peppercorns in brine,
    drained and roughly
    chopped
1 tbsp chopped fresh parsley

method

1 To prepare the lobster, remove the claws by twisting them. Crack the claws using the back of a large knife and set aside. Split the body lengthways. Remove and discard the intestinal vein, the stomach sac and the spongy gills. Remove the meat from the tail and roughly chop. Set aside with the claws.

2 Heat the oil with half the butter in a large saucepan over a medium heat. Add the onion and cook, stirring occasionally, for 5 minutes until softened. Add the garlic and cook for a further 30 seconds. Stir in the thyme. Reduce the heat, add the rice and mix to coat in butter and oil. Cook, stirring constantly, for 2–3 minutes, or until the grains are translucent.

3 Stir in the wine and cook, stirring constantly, for 1 minute until reduced. Gradually add the hot stock, a ladleful at a time. Stir constantly and add more liquid as the rice absorbs each addition. Increase the heat to medium so that the liquid bubbles. Cook for 20 minutes, or until all the liquid is absorbed and the rice is creamy. Five minutes before the end of cooking time, add the lobster meat and claws.

4 Remove the saucepan from the heat and stir in the peppercorns, remaining butter and the parsley. Spoon onto warmed plates and serve immediately.

prawn & asparagus risotto

ingredients

SERVES 4

1.2 litres/2 pints vegetable
    stock
375 g/13 oz fresh asparagus
    spears, cut into 5-cm/
    2-inch lengths
2 tbsp olive oil
1 onion, finely chopped
1 garlic clove, finely chopped
350 g/12 oz arborio rice
450 g/1 lb raw jumbo prawns,
    peeled and deveined
2 tbsp olive paste or tapenade
2 tbsp chopped fresh basil,
    plus extra to garnish
salt and pepper
fresh Parmesan cheese,
    to garnish

method

1 Bring the stock to the boil in a large saucepan. Add the asparagus and cook for 3 minutes until just tender. Strain, reserving the stock, and refresh the asparagus under cold running water. Drain and set aside. Return the stock to the saucepan and keep simmering gently over a low heat while you are cooking the risotto.

2 Heat the olive oil in a large, heavy-based saucepan. Add the onion and cook over a medium heat, stirring occasionally, for 5 minutes until softened. Add the garlic and cook for a further 30 seconds. Reduce the heat, add the rice and mix to coat in oil. Cook, stirring constantly, for 2–3 minutes, or until the grains are translucent.

3 Gradually add the hot stock, a ladleful at a time. Stir constantly and add more liquid as the rice absorbs each addition. Increase the heat to medium so that the liquid bubbles. Cook for 20 minutes, until all the liquid is absorbed and the rice is creamy. Add the prawns and asparagus when you add the last ladleful of stock.

4 Remove the saucepan from the heat, stir in the olive paste and basil and season with salt and pepper. Spoon the risotto onto warmed plates and serve immediately, garnished with Parmesan cheese and basil sprigs.

saffron & lemon risotto with scallops

ingredients

SERVES 4

16 live scallops, shucked

juice of 1 lemon, plus extra
for seasoning

3 tbsp butter

1 tbsp olive oil, plus extra for
brushing

1 small onion, finely chopped

280 g/10 oz arborio rice

1 tsp crumbled saffron
threads

1.2 litres/2 pints simmering
fish or vegetable stock

salt and pepper

2 tbsp vegetable oil

115 g/4 oz freshly grated
Parmesan or Grana
Padano cheese

1 lemon, cut into wedges and
2 tsp grated lemon rind,
to garnish

method

1 Place the scallops in a non-metallic bowl and mix with the lemon juice. Cover the bowl with clingfilm and chill for 15 minutes.

2 Melt 2 tablespoons of the butter with the oil in a deep saucepan over a medium heat. Add the onion and cook, stirring occasionally, until soft and starting to turn golden. Add the rice and mix to coat in oil and butter. Cook, stirring, until the grains are translucent. Dissolve the saffron in 4 tablespoons of hot stock and add to the rice. Gradually add the remaining stock a ladleful at a time, stirring constantly, until all the liquid is absorbed and the rice is creamy. Season with salt and pepper.

3 When the risotto is nearly cooked, preheat a griddle pan over a high heat. Brush the scallops with oil and sear on the griddle pan for 3–4 minutes on each side, depending on their thickness. Take care not to overcook or they will be rubbery.

4 Remove the risotto from the heat and add the remaining butter. Mix well, then stir in the Parmesan until it melts. Season with lemon juice, adding just 1 teaspoon at a time and tasting as you go. Serve the risotto immediately with the scallops and lemon wedges arranged on top, sprinkled with lemon zest.

prawns with coconut rice

ingredients

SERVES 4

115 g/4 oz dried Chinese
    mushrooms

2 tbsp vegetable or peanut oil

6 spring onions, chopped

55 g/2 oz dry unsweetened
    coconut

1 fresh green chilli, deseeded
    and chopped

225 g/8 oz jasmine rice

150 ml/5 fl oz fish stock

425 ml/15 fl oz coconut milk

350 g/12 oz cooked peeled
    prawns

6 sprigs fresh Thai basil

method

1 Place the mushrooms in a small bowl, cover with hot water and set aside to soak for 30 minutes. Drain, then cut off and discard the stalks and slice the caps.

2 Heat 1 tablespoon of the oil in a wok and stir-fry the spring onions, coconut and chilli for 2–3 minutes, until lightly browned. Add the mushrooms and stir-fry for 3–4 minutes.

3 Add the rice and stir-fry for 2–3 minutes, then add the stock and bring to the boil. Reduce the heat and add the coconut milk. Simmer for 10–15 minutes, until the rice is tender. Stir in the prawns and basil, heat through and serve.

smoked haddock with tagliatelle verde

ingredients

SERVES 4

450 g/1 lb smoked haddock
  fillets, skinned

280 g/10 oz dried tagliatelle
  verde

600 ml/1 pint skimmed or
  semi-skimmed milk

4 tbsp cornflour

2 shallots, finely chopped

2 tbsp snipped fresh chives

pepper

method

1 Cut the fish into chunks, removing any remaining bones.

2 Bring a large saucepan of water to the boil, add the tagliatelle and return to the boil. Cook for 8–10 minutes, or until just tender.

3 Meanwhile, blend 125 ml/4 fl oz of the milk with the cornflour in a large, heatproof bowl. Place the remaining milk in a saucepan with the shallots and bring to the boil. Pour the boiling milk over the cornflour mixture, stirring constantly. Return the milk to the saucepan and return to the boil, stirring constantly, until the sauce thickens.

4 Stir the fish into the sauce, reduce the heat to low and simmer gently for 5 minutes, or until the fish is cooked. Stir in half of the chives.

5 Drain the tagliatelle and return to the saucepan, stir in the haddock sauce and season with pepper. Serve immediately, garnished with the remaining chives.

fettuccine with smoked salmon

ingredients

SERVES 4

225 g/8 oz dried fettuccine

1 tsp olive oil

1 garlic clove, finely chopped

55 g/2 oz smoked salmon,
  cut into thin strips

55 g/2 oz watercress leaves,
  plus extra to garnish

salt and pepper

method

1 Bring a large saucepan of lightly salted water to the boil over a medium heat. Add the pasta, return to the boil and cook for 8–10 minutes, or until tender but still firm to the bite.

2 Meanwhile, heat the olive oil in a large non-stick frying pan. Add the garlic and cook over a low heat, stirring constantly, for 30 seconds. Add the salmon and watercress, season with pepper and cook for a further 30 seconds, or until the watercress has wilted.

3 Drain the cooked pasta and return to the saucepan. Mix the salmon and watercress with the pasta. Toss the mixture thoroughly using 2 large forks. Divide between 4 large serving plates and garnish with extra watercress leaves. Serve immediately.

linguine with smoked salmon & rocket

ingredients

SERVES 4

350 g/12 oz dried linguine

2 tbsp olive oil

1 garlic clove, finely chopped

115 g/4 oz smoked salmon,
    cut into thin strips

55 g/2 oz rocket

salt and pepper

lemon halves, to garnish

method

1 Bring a large, heavy-based saucepan of lightly salted water to the boil. Add the pasta, return to the boil and cook for 8–10 minutes, or until tender but still firm to the bite.

2 Just before the end of the cooking time, heat the olive oil in a heavy-based frying pan. Add the garlic and cook over a low heat, stirring constantly, for 1 minute. Do not allow the garlic to brown or it will taste bitter. Add the salmon and rocket. Season with salt and pepper and cook, stirring constantly, for 1 minute. Remove the frying pan from the heat.

3 Drain the pasta and transfer to a warmed serving dish. Add the smoked salmon and rocket mixture, toss lightly and serve, garnished with lemon halves.

macaroni & seafood bake

ingredients

SERVES 4

350 g/12 oz dried
    short-cut macaroni
6 tbsp butter, plus extra for
    greasing
2 small fennel bulbs,
    thinly sliced
175 g/6 oz mushrooms,
    thinly sliced
175 g/6 oz cooked
    peeled prawns
pinch of cayenne pepper
300 ml/10 fl oz béchamel
    sauce (see below)
55 g/2 oz freshly grated
    Parmesan cheese
2 large tomatoes, sliced
olive oil, for brushing
1 tsp dried oregano

béchamel sauce

300 ml/10 fl oz milk
1 slice of onion
1 bay leaf
6 black peppercorns
1 blade of mace
2 tbsp butter
3 tbsp plain flour
salt and pepper

method

1 To make the béchamel sauce, pour the milk into a saucepan and add the onion, bay leaf, peppercorns and mace. Heat to just below boiling point, then remove from the heat, cover, infuse for 10 minutes and strain. Melt the butter in a separate saucepan. Sprinkle in the flour and cook over a low heat, stirring constantly, for 1 minute. Gradually stir in the milk, then bring to the boil and cook, stirring, until thickened and smooth. Season to taste.

2 Bring a large saucepan of lightly salted water to the boil. Add the pasta, return to the boil and cook for 8–10 minutes, or until tender but still firm to the bite. Drain and return to the pan. Add 2 tablespoons of the butter to the pasta, cover, shake the pan and keep warm.

3 Melt the remaining butter in a saucepan. Add the fennel and cook for 3–4 minutes. Stir in the mushrooms and cook for 2 minutes. Stir in the prawns, then remove the pan from the heat. Stir the cayenne pepper into the béchamel sauce and add the prawn mixture and pasta.

4 Grease a large ovenproof dish with butter, then pour the mixture into the dish and spread evenly. Sprinkle over the Parmesan cheese and arrange the tomato slices in a ring around the edge. Brush the tomatoes with olive oil, then sprinkle over the oregano. Bake in a preheated oven, 180°C/350°F/Gas Mark 4, for 25 minutes, or until golden brown. Serve immediately.

crab ravioli

ingredients

SERVES 4

6 spring onions, plus
    shredded spring onion
    to garnish

350 g/12 oz cooked crabmeat

2 tsp finely chopped
    fresh ginger

1/8–1/4 tsp chilli or Tabasco
    sauce

700 g/1 lb 9 oz tomatoes,
    peeled, deseeded and
    roughly chopped

1 garlic clove, finely chopped

1 tbsp white wine vinegar

1 quantity basic pasta dough
    (see below)

plain flour, for dusting

1 egg, lightly beaten

salt

2 tbsp double cream

pasta dough

200 g/7 oz plain flour, plus
    extra for dusting

pinch of salt

2 eggs, lightly beaten

1 tbsp olive oil

method

1 To make the pasta dough, sift the flour into a food processor. Add the salt, eggs and olive oil and process until the dough begins to come together. Knead on a lightly floured work surface until smooth. Cover and set aside for 30 minutes.

2 Thinly slice the spring onions, keeping the white and green parts separate. Mix the green spring onions, crabmeat and ginger, with chilli sauce to taste, in a bowl. Cover and chill.

3 Process the tomatoes in a food processor to a purée. Place the garlic, white spring onions, and vinegar in a saucepan and add the puréed tomatoes. Bring to the boil, stirring, then simmer gently for 10 minutes. Remove from the heat.

4 Thinly roll out half of the pasta dough on a lightly floured work surface. Cover with a tea towel and roll out the other half. Place small mounds of the filling in rows 4 cm/1 1/2 inches apart on one sheet of dough. Brush in between with beaten egg. Cover with the other half of dough. Press down between the mounds, cut into squares and rest on a tea towel for 1 hour.

5 Bring a large saucepan of lightly salted water to the boil. Add the ravioli, in batches, return to the boil and cook for 5 minutes. Remove with a slotted spoon and drain on kitchen paper. Gently heat the tomato sauce and whisk in the cream. Serve the ravioli with the sauce poured over and garnished with shredded spring onion.

spaghetti with clams

ingredients

SERVES 4

1 kg/2 lb 4 oz live clams,
    scrubbed under cold
    running water*

175 ml/6 fl oz water

175 ml/6 fl oz dry white wine

salt and pepper

350 g/12 oz dried spaghetti

5 tbsp olive oil

2 garlic cloves, finely chopped

4 tbsp chopped fresh
    flat-leaf parsley

* discard any clams with
broken or damaged shells
and any that do not shut
when sharply tapped

method

1 Place the clams in a large, heavy-based saucepan, add the water and wine, cover and cook over a high heat, shaking the saucepan occasionally, for 5 minutes, or until the shells have opened.

2 Remove the clams with a slotted spoon and cool slightly. Strain the cooking liquid into a small saucepan through a sieve lined with muslin. Bring to the boil and cook until reduced by about half, then remove from the heat. Meanwhile, discard any clams with damaged shells or that have not opened, then remove the remainder from their shells and reserve until required.

3 Bring a large saucepan of lightly salted water to the boil. Add the pasta, return to the boil and cook for 8–10 minutes, or until tender but still firm to the bite.

4 Meanwhile, heat the olive oil in a large, heavy-based frying pan. Add the garlic and cook, stirring frequently, for 2 minutes. Add the parsley and the reduced clam cooking liquid and simmer gently.

5 Drain the pasta and add it to the frying pan with the clams. Season with salt and pepper and cook, stirring constantly, for 4 minutes, or until the pasta is coated and the clams have heated through. Transfer to a warmed serving dish and serve immediately.

fish curry with rice noodles

ingredients

SERVES 4

2 tbsp vegetable or peanut oil

1 large onion, chopped

2 garlic cloves, chopped

85 g/3 oz button mushrooms

225 g/8 oz monkfish, cut into
2.5-cm/1-inch cubes

225 g/8 oz salmon fillets, cut
into 2.5-cm/1-inch cubes

225 g/8 oz cod fillets, cut into
2.5-cm/1-inch cubes

2 tbsp Thai red curry paste

400 g/14 oz canned coconut
milk

handful of fresh coriander,
chopped

1 tsp brown sugar

1 tsp Thai fish sauce

115 g/4 oz dried rice noodles

3 spring onions, chopped

50 g/2 oz beansprouts

few fresh Thai basil leaves

method

1 Heat the oil in a preheated wok or large frying pan over a medium heat, add the onion, garlic and mushrooms and cook, stirring frequently, for 5 minutes until softened, but not browned.

2 Add the fish, curry paste and coconut milk and bring gently to the boil. Simmer for 2–3 minutes before adding half the coriander and the sugar and fish sauce. Keep warm.

3 Meanwhile, soak the noodles in enough boiling water to cover in a heatproof bowl for 3–4 minutes until tender, or cook according to the packet instructions. Drain well through a metal colander. Put the colander and noodles over a saucepan of simmering water. Add the spring onions, beansprouts and most of the basil and steam on top of the noodles for 1–2 minutes until just wilted.

4 Pile the noodles onto warmed serving plates and top with the fish curry. Sprinkle the remaining coriander and basil over the top and serve immediately.

cod with spiced noodles

ingredients

SERVES 4

1 tbsp peanut or corn oil

finely grated rind and juice of
1 large lemon

4 cod or haddock steaks,
about 140 g/5 oz each,
skinned

paprika, to taste

salt and pepper

spiced noodles

250 g/9 oz dried medium
Chinese egg noodles

1 tbsp peanut or corn oil

2 garlic cloves, chopped

2.5-cm/1-inch piece fresh
ginger, peeled and finely
chopped

2 tbsp very finely chopped
fresh coriander roots

1 tbsp kecap manis (sweet
soy sauce)

1 Thai chilli, deseeded and
finely chopped

1 tbsp nam pla
(Thai fish sauce)

method

1 Put the noodles in a saucepan of boiling water and boil for 3 minutes, until soft, or cook according to the packet instructions. Drain, rinse with cold water to stop the cooking and drain again, then set aside.

2 Mix 1 tablespoon of the oil with the lemon juice and brush over one side of each fish steak. Sprinkle with the lemon rind and a dusting of paprika and add a little salt and pepper. Lightly brush a grill rack with oil, then place the fish on the rack and grill under a grill preheated to high, about 10 cm/4 inches from the heat, for 8–10 minutes, until the flesh flakes easily.

3 Meanwhile, heat a wok or large frying pan over a high heat. Add 1 tablespoon of oil and heat until it shimmers. Add the garlic and ginger and stir-fry for about 30 seconds. Add the coriander and kecap manis and stir round. Add the noodles and stir thoroughly so they are coated in the kecap manis. Stir in the chopped chilli and nam pla. Serve each grilled fish steak on a bed of noodles.

teriyaki salmon fillets with chinese noodles

ingredients

SERVES 4

4 salmon fillets, about
200 g/7 oz each, any
scales wiped off

125 ml/4 fl oz
teriyaki marinade

1 shallot, sliced

2-cm/¾-inch piece fresh
ginger, finely chopped

2 carrots, sliced

115 g/4 oz closed-cup
mushrooms, sliced

1.2 litres/2 pints
vegetable stock

250 g/9 oz dried medium
egg noodles

115 g/4 oz frozen peas

175 g/6 oz Napa cabbage,
shredded

4 spring onions, sliced

method

1 Arrange the salmon fillets, skin-side up, in a dish just large enough to fit them in a single layer. Mix the teriyaki marinade with the shallot and ginger and pour over the fish. Cover and marinate in the refrigerator for 1 hour, turning the salmon over once.

2 Put the carrots, mushrooms and stock in a large saucepan. Arrange the salmon, skin-side down, on a shallow baking tray. Pour the fish marinade into the saucepan of vegetables and stock and bring to the boil. Reduce the heat, cover and simmer for 10 minutes.

3 Meanwhile, cook the salmon under a grill preheated to medium for 10–15 minutes, until the flesh turns pink and flakes easily. Remove from the grill and keep warm.

4 Add the noodles and peas to the stock and return to the boil. Reduce the heat, cover and simmer for 5 minutes, or until the noodles are tender. Stir in the Napa cabbage and spring onions and heat through for 1 minute.

5 Drain off 300 ml/10 fl oz of the stock into a heatproof jug and set aside. Drain and discard the remaining stock. Divide the noodles and vegetables between 4 warmed serving bowls and top each with a salmon fillet. Pour over the reserved stock and serve.

thai fisherman's catch

ingredients

SERVES 4

20 cooked jumbo prawns

20 cooked mussels in their
shells*

55 g/2 oz oyster mushrooms,
wiped

2 spring onions, finely sliced

3 kaffir lime leaves,
thinly sliced

1 lemon grass stalk, centre
part only, finely chopped

$1/2$ red onion, very thinly sliced

100 g/$3^1/2$ oz dried medium
rice noodles

thai coconut
dressing

125 ml/4 fl oz
creamed coconut

3 tbsp lime juice

$1^1/2$ tbsp nam pla (Thai fish
sauce)

$1^1/2$ tbsp brown sugar

1–2 fresh red chillies, to taste,
deseeded and thinly sliced

1 small garlic clove, crushed

* discard any mussels that
remain closed after cooking

method

1 To make the dressing, stir all the
ingredients together in a large bowl until the
sugar dissolves. Add the prawns, mussels,
mushrooms, spring onions, lime leaves, lemon
grass and red onion, then cover and chill until
required.

2 Meanwhile, soak the noodles in a bowl
with enough lukewarm water to cover for
20 minutes, until soft, or cook according to
the packet instructions. Drain well.

3 To serve, divide the noodles between 4 bowls.
Spoon the seafood salad over them, adding
any extra dressing.

malaysian-style coconut noodles with prawns

ingredients

SERVES 4

2 tbsp vegetable oil

1 small red pepper, deseeded and diced

200 g/7 oz pak choi, stalks thinly sliced and leaves chopped

2 large garlic cloves, chopped

1 tsp ground turmeric

2 tsp garam masala

1 tsp chilli powder (optional)

125 ml/4 fl oz hot vegetable stock

2 heaping tbsp smooth peanut butter

350 ml/12 fl oz coconut milk

1 tbsp soy sauce

250 g/9 oz thick rice noodles

280 g/10 oz cooked peeled jumbo prawns

2 spring onions, finely shredded and 1 tbsp sesame seeds, to garnish

method

1 Heat the oil in a preheated wok or large, heavy-based frying pan over a high heat. Add the red pepper, pak choi stalks and garlic and stir-fry for 3 minutes. Add the turmeric, garam masala, chilli powder, if using, and pak choi leaves and stir-fry for 1 minute.

2 Mix the hot stock and peanut butter together in a heatproof bowl until the peanut butter has dissolved, then add to the stir-fry with the coconut milk and soy sauce. Cook for 5 minutes over a medium heat, or until reduced and thickened.

3 Meanwhile, immerse the noodles in a bowl of just boiled water. Let stand for 4 minutes, then drain and refresh the noodles under cold running water. Add the cooked noodles and prawns to the coconut curry and cook for a further 2–3 minutes, stirring frequently, until heated through.

4 Serve the noodle dish sprinkled with spring onions and sesame seeds.

prawn laksa

ingredients

SERVES 4

20–24 large raw unpeeled
　prawns
450 ml/16 fl oz fish stock
pinch of salt
1 tsp peanut oil
450 ml/16 fl oz coconut milk
2 tsp nam pla (Thai fish sauce)
1/2 tablespoon lime juice
115 g/4 oz dried medium
　rice-flour noodles
115 g/4 oz beansprouts
fresh coriander, chopped,
　to garnish

laksa paste

6 fresh coriander stalks with
　leaves
3 large garlic cloves, crushed
1 fresh red chilli, deseeded
　and chopped
1 lemon grass stalk, centre
　part only, chopped
2.5-cm/1-inch piece fresh
　ginger, peeled and
　chopped
1 1/2 tbsp shrimp paste
1/2 tsp ground turmeric
2 tbsp peanut oil

method

1 Remove the heads and shells from the
prawns, leaving the tails intact, and devein.
Reserve the heads and shells. Put the fish
stock, salt and the prawn heads and shells in
a saucepan over a high heat and slowly bring
to the boil. Lower the heat and simmer for
10 minutes.

2 Meanwhile, make the laksa paste. Put all the
ingredients, except the oil, in a food processor
and blend. With the motor running, slowly add
up to 2 tablespoons of peanut oil just until
a paste forms. (If your food processor is too
large to work efficiently with this small quantity,
use a mortar and pestle.)

3 Heat the 1 teaspoon of peanut oil in a large
saucepan over a high heat. Add the paste and
stir-fry until it is fragrant. Strain the fish stock
through a sieve lined with muslin. Stir the stock
into the laksa paste, along with the coconut
milk, nam pla and lime juice. Bring to the boil,
then cover and simmer for 30 minutes.

4 Meanwhile, soak the noodles in a large bowl
with enough lukewarm water to cover for
20 minutes, until soft. Drain and set aside.

5 Add the prawns and beansprouts to the
soup and continue simmering just until the
prawns turn opaque and curl. Divide the
noodles between 4 bowls and ladle the soup
over. Serve garnished with chopped coriander.

scallops on noodles

ingredients

SERVES 4

115 g/4 oz dried green tea
noodles, or the thinnest
green noodles you can find

30 g/1 oz butter

1 garlic clove, crushed

pinch of paprika

1 tbsp peanut or corn oil, plus
a little extra for cooking
the scallops

2 tbsp bottled mild or medium
Thai green curry paste

2 tbsp water

2 tsp light soy sauce

2 spring onions, finely
shredded, and extra
spring onions, sliced,
to garnish

12 fresh scallops, shucked,
with shells reserved,
if possible

salt and pepper

method

1 Boil the green tea noodles for about
1¹/2 minutes, until soft, then rinse with cold
water and drain well. For any other noodles,
follow the packet instructions. Drain and set
aside. Meanwhile, melt the butter in a small
saucepan and cook the garlic in it for about
1 minute. Add the paprika and set aside.

2 Heat a wok over a high heat. Add the oil.
Stir in the curry paste, water and soy sauce
and bring to the boil. Add the noodles and
stir around to reheat. Stir in the spring onions,
then remove from the heat and keep warm.

3 Heat a ridged griddle pan over a high heat
and brush lightly with a little oil. Add the
scallops to the pan and cook for 3 minutes on
the first side, then no more than 2 minutes
on the second, brushing with the garlic butter,
until just cooked (the centre shouldn't be
totally opaque if cut open). Season with salt
and pepper. Divide the noodles between
4 serving plates and top with 3 scallops
each. Garnish with spring onions and serve
immediately.

salads & stir-fries

Salads and stir-fries are two of the most healthy ways to eat vegetables, and adding a first-class protein in the form of fish and seafood makes an ideal combination. This chapter is filled with inspiring ideas for those who have health problems, or who believe that prevention is better than cure!

Salmon & Avocado Salad, Smoked Salmon, Asparagus & Avocado Salad, Tuna & Two-bean Salad, Prawn & Papaya Salad and Monkfish Stir-fry are excellent options for maintaining a healthy heart, and diabetics can enjoy Tuna & Avocado Salad and Coconut Prawns with Cucumber Salad. Avocado, rather like oil-rich fish, is often viewed with suspicion because of its high fat content, but the fat is almost entirely monounsaturated and is excellent for the circulatory system. It also has a fabulous, smooth texture that goes very well with fresh or smoked salmon and fresh tuna, so recipes with these ingredients have a recklessly indulgent air about them and feed the soul as well as the body!

If you are not on a restricted diet and simply love salads and stir-fries, Smoked Salmon & Wild Rocket Salad has an irresistible lime-mayonnaise dressing, and Salmon & Scallops with Coriander & Lime is packed with flavour for a special occasion.

salmon & avocado salad

ingredients

SERVES 4

450 g/1 lb new potatoes

4 salmon steaks, about
115 g/4 oz each

1 avocado

juice of $\frac{1}{2}$ lemon

55 g/2 oz baby spinach leaves

125 g/4$\frac{1}{2}$ oz mixed small
salad leaves, including
watercress

4 tomatoes, cut into quarters

55 g/2 oz chopped walnuts

dressing

3 tbsp unsweetened clear
apple juice

1 tsp balsamic vinegar

pepper

method

1 Cut the new potatoes into bite-sized pieces, put into a saucepan and cover with cold water. Bring to the boil, then reduce the heat, cover and simmer for 10–15 minutes, or until just tender. Drain and keep warm.

2 Meanwhile, preheat the grill to medium. Cook the salmon steaks under the preheated grill for 10–15 minutes, depending on the thickness of the steaks, turning halfway through cooking. Remove from the grill and keep warm.

3 While the potatoes and salmon are cooking, cut the avocado in half, remove and discard the stone and peel the flesh. Cut the avocado flesh into slices and coat in the lemon juice to prevent discoloration.

4 Toss the spinach leaves and mixed salad leaves together in a large serving bowl until combined. Arrange the greens and the tomato quarters on individual serving plates.

5 Remove and discard the skin and any bones from the salmon. Flake the salmon and divide between the plates along with the potatoes. Sprinkle the walnuts over the salads.

6 To make the dressing, mix the apple juice and vinegar together in a small bowl or jug and season well with pepper. Drizzle over the salads and serve immediately.

smoked salmon, asparagus & avocado salad

ingredients

SERVES 4

200 g/7 oz asparagus spears

1 large avocado

1 tbsp lemon juice

large handful of rocket leaves

225 g/8 oz smoked salmon

1 red onion, finely sliced

1 tbsp chopped fresh flat-leaf
    parsley, plus extra sprigs
    to garnish

1 tbsp snipped fresh chives

lemon wedges, to garnish

wholemeal bread, to serve

dressing

1 garlic clove, chopped

4 tbsp extra virgin olive oil

2 tbsp white wine vinegar

1 tbsp lemon juice

pinch of sugar

1 tsp mustard

method

1 Bring a large saucepan of salted water to the boil, add the asparagus and blanch for 4 minutes. Drain and plunge into cold water, then drain again. Set aside to cool.

2 To make the dressing, combine all the dressing ingredients in a small bowl and stir together well.

3 Halve, peel and stone the avocado and cut into bite-sized pieces. Brush with the lemon juice to prevent discoloration.

4 To assemble the salad, arrange the rocket leaves on individual serving plates and top with the asparagus and avocado. Cut the smoked salmon into strips and arrange over the top of the salads, then sprinkle over the onion and herbs. Drizzle over the dressing, then garnish with parsley sprigs and lemon wedges. Serve with wholemeal bread.

smoked salmon & wild rocket salad

ingredients

SERVES 4

50 g/1³/₄ oz wild rocket leaves

1 tbsp chopped fresh flat-leaf parsley

2 spring onions, finely diced

2 large avocados

1 tbsp lemon juice

250 g/9 oz smoked salmon

lime wedges, to serve

lime mayonnaise

150 ml/5 fl oz mayonnaise

2 tbsp lime juice

finely grated rind of 1 lime

1 tbsp chopped fresh flat-leaf parsley, plus extra sprigs to garnish

method

1 Shred the rocket and arrange in 4 individual salad bowls or on 4 small plates. Sprinkle over the chopped parsley and spring onions.

2 Halve, peel and stone the avocados and cut into thin slices or small chunks. Brush with the lemon juice to prevent discoloration, then divide between the salad bowls. Mix together gently. Cut the smoked salmon into strips and sprinkle over the top.

3 Put the mayonnaise in a bowl, then add the lime juice and rind and the chopped parsley. Mix together well. Spoon some of the lime mayonnaise on top of each salad, garnish with parsley sprigs and serve with lime wedges for squeezing over.

smoked haddock salad

ingredients

SERVES 4

350 g/12 oz smoked haddock
    fillet, skinned

4 tbsp olive oil

1 tbsp lemon juice

2 tbsp soured cream

1 tbsp hot water

2 tbsp snipped fresh chives,
    plus extra to garnish

salt and pepper

1 plum tomato, peeled,
    deseeded and diced

8 quails' eggs

4 thick slices wholegrain or
    multigrain bread

115 g/4 oz mixed salad leaves

method

1 Fill a large frying pan with water and bring to the boil. Add the smoked haddock fillet, cover and remove the frying pan from the heat. Set aside for 10 minutes until the fish is tender. Remove with a slotted spoon and drain on a plate. Flake the fish, removing and discarding any small bones. Set aside. Discard the cooking liquid.

2 Meanwhile, whisk the oil, lemon juice, soured cream, hot water, chives, salt and pepper together in a bowl. Stir in the tomato. Set aside.

3 Bring a small saucepan of water to the boil. Carefully lower the quails' eggs into the water and cook for 3–4 minutes from when the water returns to the boil (3 minutes for a slightly soft centre, 4 minutes for a firm centre). Drain immediately and refresh under cold running water. Carefully shell the eggs, cut in half lengthways and set aside.

4 Toast the bread and put a slice on each of 4 serving plates. Top with the salad leaves, then the flaked fish and finally the quails' eggs. Spoon over the dressing and garnish with a few extra chives.

pasta niçoise

ingredients

SERVES 4

115 g/4 oz French beans, cut
   into 5-cm/2-inch lengths
225 g/8 oz dried fusilli tricolore
100 ml/3½ fl oz olive oil
2 tuna steaks, about
   350 g/12 oz each
salt and pepper
6 cherry tomatoes, halved
55 g/2 oz black olives, pitted
   and halved
6 canned anchovies, drained
   and chopped
3 tbsp chopped fresh
   flat-leaf parsley
2 tbsp lemon juice
8–10 radicchio leaves

method

1 Bring a large, heavy-based saucepan of lightly salted water to the boil. Add the French beans, reduce the heat and cook for 5–6 minutes. Remove with a slotted spoon and refresh in a bowl of cold water. Drain well. Add the pasta to the same saucepan, return to the boil and cook for 8–10 minutes, or until tender but still firm to the bite.

2 Meanwhile, brush a griddle pan with some of the olive oil and heat until smoking. Season the tuna with salt and pepper and brush both sides with some of the remaining olive oil. Cook over a medium heat for 2 minutes on each side, or until cooked to your liking, then remove from the griddle pan and reserve.

3 Drain the pasta well and tip it into a bowl. Add the French beans, cherry tomatoes, olives, anchovies, parsley, lemon juice and remaining olive oil and season with salt and pepper. Toss well and allow to cool. Remove and discard any skin from the tuna and slice thickly.

4 Gently mix the tuna into the pasta salad. Line a large salad bowl with the radicchio leaves, spoon in the salad and serve.

tuna & two-bean salad

ingredients

SERVES 4–6

200 g/7 oz French beans

400 g/14 oz canned small
    white beans, such as
    cannellini, rinsed and
    drained

4 spring onions, finely
    chopped

2 fresh tuna steaks, about
    225 g/8 oz each and
    2 cm/³/₄ inch thick

olive oil, for brushing

salt and pepper

250 g/9 oz cherry tomatoes,
    halved

lettuce leaves

fresh mint and parsley sprigs,
    to garnish

country-style crusty bread,
    to serve

dressing

handful of fresh mint leaves,
    shredded

handful of fresh parsley
    leaves, chopped

1 garlic clove, crushed

4 tbsp extra virgin olive oil

1 tbsp red wine vinegar

salt and pepper

method

1 First, make the dressing. Put the mint, parsley, garlic, olive oil and vinegar into a screw-top jar, add salt and pepper, secure the lid and shake until blended. Pour into a large bowl and set aside.

2 Bring a saucepan of lightly salted water to the boil. Add the French beans and cook for 3 minutes. Add the white beans and cook for another 4 minutes until the French beans are tender-crisp and the white beans are heated through. Drain well and add to the bowl with the dressing and spring onions. Toss together.

3 To cook the tuna, heat a ridged griddle pan over a high heat. Lightly brush the tuna steaks with oil, then season with salt and pepper. Cook the steaks for 2 minutes, then turn over and cook on the other side for a further 2 minutes for rare or up to 4 minutes for well done.

4 Remove the tuna from the griddle pan and rest for 2 minutes, or until completely cool. When ready to serve, add the tomatoes to the bean mixture and toss lightly. Line a serving platter with lettuce leaves and pile on the bean salad. Flake the tuna over the top. Serve warm or at room temperature with plenty of bread, garnished with the herbs.

tuna & avocado salad

ingredients

SERVES 4

2 avocados, stoned, peeled
    and cubed

250 g/9 oz cherry tomatoes,
    halved

2 red peppers, deseeded and
    chopped

1 bunch fresh flat-leaf
    parsley, chopped

2 garlic cloves, crushed

1 fresh red chilli, deseeded
    and finely chopped

juice of $1/2$ lemon

6 tbsp olive oil

pepper

3 tbsp sesame seeds

4 fresh tuna steaks, about
    150 g/5$1/2$ oz each

8 cooked new potatoes, cubed

rocket leaves, to serve

method

1 Toss the avocados, tomatoes, red peppers, parsley, garlic, chilli, lemon juice and 2 tablespoons of the oil together in a large bowl. Season with pepper, cover and chill in the refrigerator for 30 minutes.

2 Lightly crush the sesame seeds in a mortar with a pestle. Tip the crushed seeds onto a plate and spread out. Press each tuna steak in turn into the crushed seeds to coat on both sides.

3 Heat 2 tablespoons of the remaining oil in a frying pan, add the potatoes and cook, stirring frequently, for 5–8 minutes, or until crisp and brown. Remove from the frying pan and drain on kitchen paper.

4 Wipe out the frying pan, add the remaining oil and heat over a high heat until very hot. Add the tuna steaks and cook for 3–4 minutes on each side.

5 To serve, divide the avocado salad between 4 serving plates. Top each with a tuna steak, then sprinkle over the potatoes and a handful of rocket leaves.

seafood & spinach salad

ingredients

SERVES 4

500 g/1 lb 2 oz live mussels,
    prepared (see page 32)
100 g/3¹/₂ oz raw prawns,
    peeled and deveined
350 g/12 oz live scallops,
    shucked and cleaned
500 g/1 lb 2 oz baby spinach
    leaves
4 tbsp water
3 spring onions, sliced
lemon wedges, to garnish

dressing

4 tbsp extra virgin olive oil
2 tbsp white wine vinegar
1 tbsp lemon juice
1 tsp finely grated lemon rind
1 garlic clove, chopped
1 tbsp grated fresh ginger
1 small fresh red chilli,
    deseeded and sliced
1 tbsp chopped fresh
    coriander, plus extra
    sprigs to garnish
salt and pepper

method

1 Put the mussels in a large saucepan with a little water and cook, covered, over a high heat, shaking the pan occasionally, for 3–4 minutes, or until the mussels have opened. Discard any mussels that remain closed. Strain the mussels, reserving the cooking liquid.

2 Return the reserved cooking liquid to the saucepan and bring to the boil, then add the prawns and scallops and cook for 3 minutes. Remove from the heat and drain. Remove the mussels from their shells. Refresh the mussels, prawns and scallops under cold running water, drain, and put them in a large bowl to cool. Cover with clingfilm and chill in the refrigerator for 45 minutes.

3 Meanwhile, rinse the spinach leaves and put them in a saucepan with the water. Cook over a high heat for 1 minute. Transfer to a colander, refresh under cold running water and drain.

4 To make the dressing, combine all the dressing ingredients in a small bowl. Divide the spinach between 4 serving dishes, then sprinkle over half the spring onions. Top with the mussels, prawns and scallops, then sprinkle over the remaining spring onions. Drizzle over the dressing, garnish with coriander sprigs and lemon wedges and serve.

coconut prawns with cucumber salad

ingredients

SERVES 4

200 g/7 oz brown basmati rice

$^{1}/_{2}$ tsp coriander seeds

2 egg whites, lightly beaten

100 g/3$^{1}/_{2}$ oz dry unsweetened coconut

24 raw jumbo prawns, peeled and tails left intact

$^{1}/_{2}$ cucumber

4 spring onions, thinly sliced

1 tsp sesame oil

1 tbsp finely chopped fresh coriander

1 lime, cut into wedges, to garnish

method

1 Bring a large saucepan of water to the boil, add the rice and cook for 25 minutes, or until tender. Drain and set aside in a sieve covered with a clean tea towel to absorb the steam.

2 Meanwhile, soak 8 wooden skewers in cold water for 30 minutes, then drain. Crush the coriander seeds in a mortar with a pestle. Heat a non-stick frying pan over a medium heat and cook the seeds, turning, until they start to colour. Tip onto a plate and set aside.

3 Put the egg whites into a shallow bowl and the coconut into a separate bowl. Roll each prawn first in the egg whites, then in the coconut. Thread onto a skewer. Repeat so that each skewer is threaded with 3 coated prawns.

4 Using a potato peeler, peel long strips from the cucumber to create ribbons, put into a sieve to drain, then toss with the spring onions and oil in a bowl and set aside.

5 Cook the prawns under a grill preheated to high for 3–4 minutes on each side, or until pink and slightly browned. Mix the rice with the coriander seeds and coriander, press into 4 dariole moulds and invert each mould onto a serving plate. Serve with cucumber salad and prawn skewers, garnished with lime wedges.

prawn & rice salad

ingredients

SERVES 4

175 g/6 oz mixed long-grain
and wild rice
350 g/12 oz cooked peeled
prawns
1 mango, peeled, stoned
and diced
4 spring onions, sliced
25 g/1 oz slivered almonds
1 tbsp finely chopped fresh
mint
pepper

dressing

1 tbsp extra virgin olive oil
2 tsp lime juice
1 garlic clove, crushed
1 tsp honey
salt and pepper

method

1 Bring a large saucepan of lightly salted water
to the boil. Add the rice, return to the boil and
cook for 35 minutes, or until tender. Drain,
then transfer to a large bowl and stir in the
prawns.

2 To make the dressing, combine the olive
oil, lime juice, garlic and honey in a large jug,
season with salt and pepper and whisk until
well blended. Pour the dressing over the rice
and prawn mixture and set aside to cool.

3 Add the mango, spring onions, almonds
and mint to the cooled salad and season with
pepper. Stir thoroughly, transfer to a large
serving dish and serve.

prawn & papaya salad

ingredients

SERVES 4

1 papaya, peeled
350 g/12 oz large cooked
    peeled prawns
assorted baby salad leaves,
    to serve

dressing

4 spring onions, finely
    chopped
2 fresh red chillies, deseeded
    and finely chopped
1 tsp fish sauce
1 tbsp vegetable or peanut oil
juice of 1 lime
1 tsp soft light brown sugar

method

1 Scoop the seeds out of the papaya and slice thinly. Stir gently together with the prawns.

2 Mix the spring onions, chillies, fish sauce, oil, lime juice and sugar together.

3 Arrange the salad leaves in a bowl and top with the papaya and prawns. Pour the dressing over and serve immediately.

monkfish stir-fry

ingredients

SERVES 4

2 tsp sesame oil

450 g/1 lb monkfish steaks, cut
    into 2.5-cm/1-inch chunks

1 red onion, thinly sliced

3 cloves garlic, finely chopped

1 tsp grated fresh ginger

225 g/8 oz fine tip asparagus

175 g/6 oz mushrooms, thinly
    sliced

2 tbsp soy sauce

1 tbsp lemon juice

lemon wedges, to garnish

cooked noodles, to serve

method

1 Heat the oil in a frying pan over a medium–
high heat. Add the fish, red onion, garlic,
ginger, asparagus and mushrooms. Stir-fry for
2–3 minutes.

2 Stir in the soy sauce and lemon juice and
cook for another minute. Remove from the
heat and transfer to warmed serving dishes.

3 Garnish with lemon wedges and serve
immediately on a bed of cooked noodles.

stir-fried rice noodles with marinated fish

ingredients

SERVES 4

450 g/1 lb monkfish or cod, cubed

225 g/8 oz salmon fillets, cubed

115 g/4 oz wide rice noodles

2 tbsp vegetable or peanut oil

2 shallots, sliced

2 garlic cloves, finely chopped

1 fresh red chilli, deseeded and chopped

2 tbsp Thai soy sauce

2 tbsp chilli sauce

sprigs of coriander, to garnish

marinade

2 tbsp vegetable or peanut oil

2 fresh green chillies, deseeded and chopped

grated rind and juice of 1 lime

1 tbsp fish sauce

method

1 Place the fish in a shallow bowl. To make the marinade, mix the oil, green chillies, lime juice and rind, and fish sauce together and pour over the fish. Cover and chill for 2 hours.

2 Put the noodles in a bowl and cover with boiling water. Leave for 8–10 minutes (check the packet instructions) and drain well.

3 Heat the oil in a wok or large frying pan and sauté the shallots, garlic and red chilli until lightly browned. Add the soy sauce and chilli sauce. Add the fish and the marinade to the wok and stir-fry gently for 2–3 minutes until cooked through.

4 Add the drained noodles and stir gently. Garnish with coriander and serve immediately.

prawn, mangetout & cashew nut stir-fry

ingredients

SERVES 4

85 g/3 oz dry roasted cashew nuts

3 tbsp peanut oil

4 spring onions, finely sliced

2 celery sticks, thinly sliced

3 carrots, finely sliced

100 g/3^1/$_2$ oz baby corn, halved

175 g/6 oz mushrooms, finely sliced

1 clove of garlic, roughly chopped

450 g/1 lb raw prawns, peeled

1 tsp cornflour

2 tbsp soy sauce

50 ml/2 fl oz chicken stock

225 g/8 oz Savoy cabbage, shredded

175 g/6 oz mangetout

cooked rice, to serve

method

1 Put a frying pan over a medium heat and add the cashew nuts; toast them until they begin to brown. Remove with a slotted spoon and reserve.

2 Add the oil to the saucepan and heat. Add the spring onions, celery, carrots and baby corn and cook, stirring occasionally, over a medium–high heat for 3–4 minutes.

3 Add the mushrooms and cook until they become brown. Mix in the garlic and prawns, stirring until the prawns turn pink.

4 Mix the cornflour smoothly with the soy sauce and chicken stock. Add the liquid to the prawn mixture and stir. Then add the Savoy cabbage, mangetout and all but a few of the cashew nuts and cook for 2 minutes.

5 Garnish with the reserved cashew nuts and serve on a bed of rice.

salmon & scallops with coriander & lime

ingredients

SERVES 4

6 tbsp peanut oil

280 g/10 oz salmon steak, skinned and cut into 2.5-cm/1-inch chunks

225 g/8 oz scallops

3 carrots, thinly sliced

2 celery sticks, cut into 2.5-cm/1-inch pieces

2 orange peppers, thinly sliced

175 g/6 oz oyster mushrooms, thinly sliced

1 clove garlic, crushed

6 tbsp chopped fresh coriander

3 shallots, thinly sliced

2 limes, juiced

1 tsp grated lime rind

1 tsp dried red pepper flakes

3 tbsp dry sherry

3 tbsp soy sauce

cooked noodles, to serve

method

1 In a wok or large frying pan, heat the oil over a medium heat. Add the salmon and scallops and stir-fry for 3 minutes. Remove from the pan, then set aside and keep warm.

2 Add the carrots, celery, peppers, mushrooms and garlic to the wok and stir-fry for 3 minutes. Add the coriander and shallots, and stir.

3 Add the lime juice and rind, dried red pepper flakes, sherry and soy sauce and stir. Return the salmon and scallops to the wok and stir-fry carefully for another minute.

4 Serve immediately on a bed of cooked noodles.

scallops in black bean sauce

ingredients

SERVES 4

2 tbsp vegetable or peanut oil

1 tsp finely chopped garlic

1 tsp finely chopped fresh ginger

1 tbsp fermented black beans, rinsed and lightly mashed

400 g/14 oz scallops

1/2 tsp light soy sauce

1 tsp Shaoxing rice wine

1 tsp sugar

3–4 red Thai chillies, finely chopped

1–2 tsp chicken stock

1 tbsp finely chopped spring onions

method

1 In a preheated wok or deep saucepan, heat the oil. Add the garlic and stir, then add the ginger and stir-fry together for about 1 minute, or until fragrant.

2 Mix in the black beans, then toss in the scallops and stir-fry for 1 minute. Add the light soy sauce, Shaoxing, sugar and chillies.

3 Lower the heat and simmer for 2 minutes, adding the stock if necessary. Finally add the spring onions, then stir and serve.

squid & red onion stir-fry

ingredients

SERVES 4

450 g/1 lb squid rings

2 tbsp plain flour

1/2 tsp salt

1 green pepper

2 tbsp peanut oil

1 red onion, sliced

160-g/5³/₄-oz jar black
    bean sauce

method

1 Rinse the squid rings under cold running water and pat dry with kitchen paper.

2 Place the flour and salt in a bowl and mix together. Add the squid rings and toss until they are finely coated.

3 Using a sharp knife, seed the pepper and slice into thin strips.

4 Heat the peanut oil in a large preheated wok. Add the pepper and red onion to the wok and stir-fry for 2 minutes, or until the vegetables are just beginning to soften. Add the squid rings and cook for a further 5 minutes, or until the squid is cooked through.

5 Add the black bean sauce to the wok and heat through until the juices are bubbling. Transfer to warmed bowls and serve immediately.